to: Mum

Happy Christmas 1993!

Love,
Christopher.

TO BUILD THE SECOND CITY

TO BUILD THE SECOND CITY

Architects and Craftsmen of Georgian Bristol

TIMOTHY MOWL

with photographs by
Gordon Kelsey

REDCLIFFE
Bristol

First published in 1991 by
Redcliffe Press Ltd,
49 Park Street, Bristol

ISBN 1 872971 26 1

Typeset and printed by
The Longdunn Press Ltd, Bristol

Contents

To Mike Jenner and Andor Gomme
who went this way before me
and cut down most of the brambles
from my path

Preface

Writing a book about a great mercantile city with an historic past, I have naturally leaned heavily on several important texts. John Latimer I discovered first in the Cathedral commemorated by a suitably erudite Edwardian monument, then I absorbed his *Annals of Bristol* for the social history any book of this nature requires. A chance purchase of a second-hand copy of C. F. W. Dening's study of the 18th century architecture of Bristol set me onto buildings since blitzed and Walter Ison's *Georgian Buildings of Bristol* was invaluable for rate-book references and lease-holders' stipulations. Finally, my constant companion for the last six months has been Gomme, Jenner and Little's *Bristol: an architectural history*. For their informed research and sensitively written accounts of my chosen period, I have dedicated this present book to Mike Jenner and Andor Gomme.

All the photographs have been specially taken by Gordon Kelsey whose patience with a perfectionist author has resulted in just the illustrative coverage I wanted to point up the text. Appreciation of architecture depends upon a seeing eye and a sensitive lens; Gordon has both.

I should like to make special mention of Julian Self who drew the ground plans and gave me the benefit of his wide knowledge of 18th century decoration; Nicholas Kingsley who was particularly helpful on Gloucestershire architectural practice; Michael Liversidge whose unravelling of the influences on the creation of the Royal Fort became, for us both, a consuming interest, and Francis Greenacre, Fine Art Curator at the City Art Gallery, who put me on to views of the city and its buildings that I would have missed. My thanks go also to the staff of the City Reference Library, Fine Art Library, the Record Office and to Nick Lee of the University Special Collections department.

Let me now thank, in no other order than the alphabetical, the following for their information, their help and their advice: Geoffrey Beard, Sir Brooke Boothby, James Bruges, Annie Burnside, Tristram Clarke, Howard Colvin, Mrs Denney, James Douet, Duncan Furber, Liz Golding, Mr Hallett, Stewart Harding, Colin Harvey, Charles Hind, David Lambert, Carol Lear, Robert Lee, Janet Margrie, Christopher Marsden-Smedley, Douglas Merritt, Elizabeth Ogborn, David Pope, Gordon Priest, Michela Rausa, Reg Redwood, Jeanne Ryder, Peggy Stembridge, Peter Ware, Robert Warin, Roger White, John Winstone.

My publisher, John Sansom, safe in his Thomas Paty eyrie above Park Street and with 90 Bristol titles to his credit, had the vision to see that a book on this period was still needed. Maureen Barton typed it flawlessly, ably supported by her husband Reg. My wife Wendy and son Adam were characteristically understanding when I was forced to swap the cook's apron for the note-pad and fountain pen.

Finally, this book could never have been written without the help of my usual co-

7

author Brian Earnshaw who accompanied me in endless walks around the city and whose enthusiasm and perceptive insights made the work a constant pleasure.

Tim Mowl, Melrose Cottages, Cotham, Spring 1991

Introduction

Asked which city, Bath or Bristol, had the wider range and variety of fine classical building, most people, Bristolians included, would answer 'Bath'. And they would be wrong. Bristol in general, Clifton in glorious particular, are the unexplored, undervalued treasure houses of 18th century design. The reason for the neglect is the paradoxical one that most of their 'Georgian' architecture was built in the 19th century when Sailor William and the young Victoria were on the throne.

Bristol never fits tidily into the usual categories. Its good fortune was to have been rich, conservative and philistine. This meant that there was ample money for lavish construction and that the classical tradition was allowed to develop to an extraordinary flowering long after it had withered in the rest of the country. Architects were left to please themselves with virtually no well-meaning patrons to restrain their imagination and experiment.

Admittedly the city made a slow start. Trapped at the beginning of the 18th century in a nonconformist brick classicism, it marked time while the rest of the country was exploring Palladian grandiosity. It was only when the brass founders and slave traders discovered the twin delights of the Rococo and the Gothick that playfully elegant villas and appalling Otrantesque castles of black slag began to appear.

Bristol was snatched from escapist fantasy and brought to creative realism by the extreme corruption of the city's self-appointed administrators. The drunken and incompetent oligarchy which claimed to control the affairs of the city had alienated its natural middle-class supporters to such an extent that, in 1831, Bristol was torched by a mob of colliers in what, at the time, looked like a dress rehearsal for a British Revolution. As a result, the prosperous classes took to the hills and created for themselves a superb classical ghetto poised on the edge of the Gorge and the Downs. So much that was good went up in a few short decades that architectural historians have never quite disentangled the figures and the forces that raised it all.

I have made major re-attributions of key buildings and sometimes radically revised a timetable of development, but what mattered ultimately was personality. If this book has captured the nature of Bristol's chief architects and craftsmen, it has succeeded. The tentative subversions of John Strahan, the undirected brilliance of the Paty team, Charles Dyer's decisive generosity, Underwood's neurotic minimalism and the awful spiritual vacancy of Richard Shackleton Pope – these created the complex fabric of the city and these have been my text.

ONE

Quaker Brick and Scottish Stone

In 1711 two substantial houses were being completed in Bristol, one down in the city in Queen Square, the other upon Clifton Green. Both had been designed for men anxious to cut more than the usual architectural figure. The first, No.29 Queen Square, was brick fronted; the other up in Clifton, known now as the Bishop's House, was of stone. Between them they illustrate precisely the damaging schism that had struck the city's building industry as a result of an ill-considered scheme floated by a debt-ridden Council in the last months of the old century.

Most English city corporations in the 17th century were self-interested, drunken and profligate. But the Council of Bristol had a head start on all the others by the city's shipping links with the wine, sherry and (after the Methuen Treaty[1]) port-producing areas of Western Europe. As a result, Bristol hospitality was infamous. Even Pepys was staggered. Judges and visiting dignitaries were inundated with alcohol. Barrels served as bribes. When war was declared on France the aldermen and their cronies visited six taverns that evening and drank two gallons (not pints) of sherry in each. Trips to outlying manorial courts like Portishead became well-organised pub crawls. Even a duck-shoot on the mill pond where the Bathurst Basin now lies was alcoholic, with the aldermen at more risk than the ducks.

But as the debts mounted there were serious cutbacks. The Mayor's allowance had been clipped by fifty guineas. The two city MPs lost their parliamentary attendance of 6s.8d. a day. Judges were denied their usual hospitality: 'not from want of respect, but pure necessity.'[2] Even the silver trumpets, that were the regular musical accompaniment to civic pomps, had to be sold and replaced by the inferior tone of copper.

Faced with these threats to their outrageously inflated life-style, the Council looked around for a saviour. Inevitably that saviour was John Romsey, the Town Clerk. He had held office, with a brief interruption in 1688, from 1676 and would continue in it until 1720. By sheer longevity and hard political experience he was a more potent figure in the city than any short-tenured mayor or sheriff. It was Romsey who had thought up the unscrupulous device in 1687 to fleece rich Quakers by offering them a high civic office which they were then obliged to refuse because their religion forbade the swearing of oaths. The resultant fines that were imposed on them had left the Council at least £1,900 better off. But in 1699, with debts of £16,000 that their entire annual income could barely service, the Council turned to Romsey again.

This time his solution appeared even more ingenious and it would, in fact, clear the outstanding debts within ten years. It gave a select number of aldermen and councillors a chance to make a good investment and it gave Bristol, if Lincoln's Inn Fields is excepted, the largest urban square in Britain. There were just two casualties. First were the citizenry who had enjoyed playing bowls on a recreational area called the Marsh, south of King Street. Second was the natural evolution of classical architecture in Bristol and the resultant yawning stylistic gap between the quality of No.29 Queen Square and that of the Bishop's House.

On 23 October 1699 Romsey and his business crony, the Mayor, a draper called John Bachelor, put to the Council a proposal to sell off building plots on the Marsh on leases of five lives, which were soon altered to fifty-three years. A peppercorn rent would be paid for the first two years while a house was being built. Thereafter a yearly ground rent of a shilling per foot of the frontage of the house would ensure the Council a steady income. The terms must have been carefully calculated for they were eagerly accepted. A reigning Sheriff, James Hollidge, and three subsequent mayors of Bristol joined the rush to take out leases, often for more than one house. It was clear, therefore, who was meant to benefit. Bristol Council in 1699 was still a tight little band. Under Romsey's often devious leadership they had all passed through political hell and high water in the brief, troubled reign of James II. Now the good times were on the way back. When 1714 came and the Council felt constrained to celebrate the accession of German George, they were able to set to with all their old tipsy abandon: fifty-three gallons of port and fifteen each of sherry and claret were swilled down, thanks to ground rents.

What was revolutionary and destructive about their venture was the stipulation in each lease that the fronts of the houses should be built of brick with quoins of freestone and a wooden modillion cornice. In 1699 brick facades were virtually unknown in the city. There was only one brick kiln, across the river at Cold Harbour, producing material for flues and chimneys. Stonemasons working the rough local Pennant sandstone and carpenters using timber and plaster had the monopoly of building operations. Now, at a stroke, John Romsey had broken that hold and handed over the city's prestige housing site to a workforce untrained in their medium and using bricks of inferior quality. It is not easy at this distance in time to assess his motives.

Romsey may have had a friend who owned a brick kiln. That would have been very Bristolian. He may, on the other hand, have hoped to introduce London building standards to his native city. He visited the capital each year on civic business, bribing a secretary or that secretary's secretary with cases of sherry or with gold coins. So he would have observed the spectacular achievements of a shady speculative builder, Dr. Nicholas Barbon, who had raised whole neighbourhoods of brick houses, all at cut prices, and designed to standard patterns.[3] Mincing Lane, Buckingham Street and Newport Square were just a few of the Barbon builds. The Doctor had studied for his degree in Leyden and his London streets were a copy of the cheaper middle-class housing of that city and of Utrecht. But London had, like Holland, a long tradition of making, cutting and laying bricks. Bristol, as the bricks and mortaring of surviving houses in Queen Square proves, had none of this.

Romsey's leases were not limited to stipulating the materials of the houses. They

11

also dictated their proportions. After an early experiment with four storey houses (a gaunt, uneasy specimen survives as No.53 Queen Charlotte Street) Romsey altered the requirement for houses actually built in the new square to one of three storeys with a ground floor of eleven feet, a first floor of ten feet and a second floor of nine feet. There is a relatively unaltered example, No.36, at the corner of Grove Avenue. It is a plain, decent house and on a village green might be termed handsome, but it is hardly worth a second glance.

This is the unfortunate reality that tends to be discreetly glossed over when Queen Square is mentioned. It is certainly an ambitious space, and Rysbrack's statue of King William that rides with such casual elegance in the centre is great art, but the houses themselves are unworthy. They are a haphazard mix of three and five-bay structures with no pattern to the placing of the doors and no bold projecting features to articulate the sprawling lengths. To describe them as 'baroque' makes a mockery of the term. They have neither movement nor power. Romsey brought to the city a medium its craftsmen had not mastered and could only deploy in the most basic elevations. He brought it too at a dead time, a lull between styles, when the Carolean had lost whatever impetus it may have possessed and when the Palladian revival was only a gleam in the eyes of a few Scots. Great individual architects of this period were two-a-penny: Wren, Vanbrugh, Archer, Hawksmoor and Talman, but an accepted national style had not evolved.

The men who raised Queen Square for the lessees were house-carpenters like John Price and Peter Wilkins, feeling their way in the new medium and permitted to build a few smaller units themselves to sell for a profit. With John Price, and serving his carpenter's apprenticeship, was the young Quaker, George Tully, who was to become extraordinarily influential, considering his modest talents, in shaping the face of the city until his death in 1770. By that time he had laid out Dowry, King and Brunswick Squares and built many houses himself.

That was the danger with Queen Square. It was not an experimental one-off, but became a template to guide and limit the city for decades to come. Where Bath leapt forward, Bristol hung modestly back, satisfied with its plain, Anglo-Dutch compromise. It is hard to resist the suggestion that those 'flat Stuart' facades satisfied something self-denying and non-conformist in a city where Quakers had been given, in 1698, the right to become burgesses by affirmation instead of by swearing. John Romsey was, as his superb, three-legged silver candlesticks in the cathedral testify, a High Churchman. But, perhaps inadvertently, he endowed Bristol with a house-style peculiarly appropriate to nonconformity.

To return to No.29 Queen Square, the house tries desperately to deny its Quaker-plain, basic shape. It is a fascinating design, clear proof that brick was not satisfying the aspirations of at least one lessee. Over an exterior of rough bricks with window lintels of well-cut gauged brickwork, the builder has applied no fewer than four separate sets of columns of the three orders, none of them supporting even a cornice, let alone a pediment. Yet nine small pediments sit without visible means of support on as many window lintels and in the middle of each lintel, like monsters strayed from a Jacobean timber-framed house in the old city, is a grotesque head grinning at the architectural jokes that are being played around it.

It is an elevation with all the charm of untutored enthusiasm, a memory perhaps of the first pages of a pattern book or some Oxford college gateway of the 1630s. In no way is it urban design for the 18th century. Inside the house a flat elliptical arch spans the wide hall grandly before a fine staircase with the standard three twisted balusters to a tread and well carved risers. With raised-and-fielded panelling in the grand rooms it has survived, not by a miracle, but by being turned into a home for old sailors.

No.29 Queen Square was put together by a good house-carpenter with the lessee breathing down his neck demanding more enrichments. The Bishop's House, its exact contemporary upon the hill, was designed by an architect using limestone and served by masons who knew their craft. Before that architect is dismissed as one of modest talents, the year of its completion, 1711, should be remembered. If this is not a Palladian villa with the correct bay rhythm of 1/3/1, a rusticated ground floor with the piano nobile on the first floor and each window set as an isolated incident in a smooth sea of ashlar, then it is a remarkably close approach to one. Its bay rhythm is 2/1/2; the central bay with the doorway breaks forward and is rusticated; the windows are isolated in the smooth ashlar walls of the side bays, but they are segmental-headed not Palladian. Only the small window above the door has a triangular pediment. The door is set between fluted Ionic pilasters that carry a burly segmental pediment. Hovering on the edge of Palladian conviction, but made slightly sullen by that baroque concentration of interest on the central bay, the whole composition is topped by an elegant balustraded parapet with urns and enclosed between banded pilasters.

For brick-bound Bristol in 1711 it was a prodigy and for England in general at that date it was experimental. Who then was its architect? Here it is necessary to tread carefully as the Bishop's House is almost certainly the first work in the city of John Strahan and he, on no more authority than that of his professional rival John Wood, is not supposed to have arrived in Bristol until 1725.

It is not simply that every feature of this Clifton villa is re-used in a slightly more sophisticated way on houses that can be confidently ascribed to Strahan, numbers 68 and 70 Prince Street, but the architect took a particular pleasure in contrasted planes of recessed stonework. This reached a peak of subtlety in his last work, the Redland Chapel of 1740–3, and it appears in one significant recurring motif of his house elevations which is virtually unique to Strahan and a signature, therefore, of his designing hand. The Bishop's House has it. It is a framing band of raised stone running below the cornice as a connecting extension from the topmost quoin of one banded pilaster strip to the other. Not easy to describe and almost subliminal in effect, it is the device of a highly sensitive architect anxious to control and stress the unity of his elevations.

Strahan appears to have been a Scot, and Scotland at exactly this time had the

13

edge on England in the move to correct Palladianism. Colen Campbell, the apostle of the revival, was also a Scot. Shiercliff, writing in 1789, credited Strahan with Redland Court, which he designed in 1735, and 'many other capital mansions in and near Bristol'.[4] These certainly include Frampton Court of 1731-3, built for Richard Clutterbuck, the Bristol Controller of Customs, and probably Cleve Hill of about 1723, both near Bristol.[5] It now seems that the Bishop's House is one of Strahan's hitherto forgotten 'capital mansions' in Bristol itself: a villa before its time from a Scot who had come riding down to stir up the architectural ambitions of a backward but rich provincial city. Venice built the country retreats of its merchant grandees out on the banks of the Brenta. The Avon was too soiled with commerce so the Bishop's House became the nucleus of Bristol's own Fiesole or Frascati up there on the Clifton heights.

In 1723 George Tully rebuilt the house of Thomas Goldney the younger immediately across the road from the Bishop's House. This, the second villa on the hill, was again of stone, not brick, a grand but conservative house with the old-fashioned baroque emphasis on the central bay. Its garden front has survived Alfred Waterhouse's 19th century additions, the east wing intact, the west sensitively refaced. From cornice to the ground its first and ground floor windows are connected by the usual baroque extrusions.

What has diverted attention from the innovatory importance of the Bishop's House is not Goldney but Clifton Hill House. That immaculately restrained and utterly correct Palladian villa was designed in 1746 by Isaac Ware, a paragon of the Burlingtonian form, only a few yards down the slope. The Bishop's House sits aslant at the top of Constitution Hill as if politely averting its eyes from a superior sister. But it had led the way a full thirty-five years earlier and begun that remarkable binary unity that tends now to be mentioned in one breath: 'Bristol and Clifton.' The ambitious stone villas up on the hill would rise in the 19th century to an amazing climax of uninhibited classicism, while in the sober brick terraces down below a more plodding and commercial destiny would be worked out.

It would appear perverse in an account of Bristol classicism to bypass John Vanbrugh's Kings Weston House (1712-14), a house of such emphatic character and less than four miles from the city centre. The truth is that, apart from chimneys at Bishopsworth Manor and some minor details of the Redland Chapel, it had no influence on the city.[6] Brilliantly but idiosyncratically baroque on its east front, Palladian in its reference on the south, Kings Weston was itself a house on the cusp, caught in stylistic indecision and presenting, therefore, no obvious model to follow. Merchants might look to a gentry house like Strahan's Cleve Hill for an example but not to a gargantuan villa breathing 'expense' from every massive architrave and ponderous cornice. As Brewer wrote much later in 1825, 'with most spectators the exterior will rather be approved than admired.' If the stir of its construction attracted John Strahan down initially from Scotland that was its only service to Bristol. The city went its own excessively modest way.

St. James's Square, lost now by war and planning policy, was built quickly by private enterprise between 1707 and 1716, while the far larger Queen Square was still going up. This was Queen Square all over again, but in miniature; the same flat brick facades with alternate quoining between each house, old-fashioned shell hoods over the doorways and flat lintels to the windows. There was even a repeat of the columns of the orders from No.29 on one house. A simple pedimented feature linking two houses on the east side did mark an advance on its original. But Queen Square had, between 1710 and 1711, gained its own off-centre controlling feature in the Customs House on a high, Ionic colonnade. This was built for the Corporation by John Hollidge, a relative of the ex-Sheriff, at a cost of £2,525 but it brought in a yearly rental of £120 to swell the drinking fund.

The next money-raising enterprise was Orchard Street. This, against all the odds, remains with us, claustrophic but genteel, jostled by the loutish bulk of warehouses and a precious evocation of both the graces and the harsh practicalities attendant on the lives of 18th century merchants. It has been limewashed but underneath it is Queen Square once more, red brick with stone quoins.

Here again John Romsey has made his mark. He was still in office on 18 January 1718 when the first leases were signed. A new clause demanding that the walls be 'carried up above the Eves of the houses and no Mundilians or Coves shall be made'[7] proves that he was in touch as ever with the housing scene of London, where a statute of 1707 had forbidden wooden modillion cornices as a fire precaution. Peter Wilkins and John Price were building again. Price raised seven of the houses, five of them on the north side of Orchard Street. In the leases for numbers 25 and 26 he persuaded Romsey to change the stipulations for the respective heights of the first and ground floors to make the first floor a foot higher. That may well have been a move towards the grander piano nobile of Palladian practice.

Inside another house on the street, No.28, there are two richly carved door surrounds, one set above the other at the top and bottom of a fine, conventional staircase of the period. It is noticeable that the upper Corinthian arch has a more impressively carved spandrel than the Ionic arch on the ground floor so there too the grander rooms may have been moving up a floor.

So far, in all these brick developments, and Orchard Street was not completed until 1722, there had been only halting movements towards a terrace, that essential concept in ambitious urban planning. When three five-bay houses like numbers thirty-six, thirty-eight and forty Queen Square were built side by side, there was a certain natural linkage by the continuous modillion cornice. There was also that shared pediment in St. James's Square. But Bristolians loved their demarcation lines, their bands of quoining, alternate or pilastered, their 'lesenes' that emphasised separateness and were usually the only effective patterning on those blank brick frontages. It is significant, therefore, that the first conscious linkage of three houses to form at least a proto-terrace was carried out in stone where the architect could rely on his masons to construct the decorative linking features with easy competence.

This was in Redcross Street, far from the restraints of Queen Square. There, if 'baroque' can be interpreted to include a design where the several main elements are visually 'connected', stands the dramatic relic of a baroque terrace. It is less overtly classical in its elements than the Bishop's House with no pediments or pilasters, only fine ashlar and panels of raised stone to link each of its window bays in vertical tiers. George Tully's garden front to Goldney House is articulated in the same simple way and Redcross Street may well be his work.[8] Skelton recorded the place in its prime when there were smaller, two-and-a-half-bay houses built like wings, one on each side of the surviving five-bay centrepiece. A recent planning compromise has subjected the survivor to a meticulous restoration but clamped two blocks of maroon coloured concrete against it like brutalist ear muffs to a delicate face. It deserves a visit for the Piranesian grotesquerie of the juxtaposition.

At this point it is worth noting that ecclesiastical design in Bristol was never blighted as domestic design had been by Romsey's leases and the imposed reign of brick. The Established Church was better armoured against nonconformist influences than the City Council. The term 'baroque' can be applied without any of the usual reservations to the ironwork screens of several city churches, to George Townesend's octagon and cupola of 1716–17 that rises with such confidence on All Saints' square tower, and above all to the superb reredos of 1716 in St. Thomas's church.

This last, almost continental, devotional artefact, is made of Flemish oak. Its richly fluted Corinthian columns break out from Corinthian pilasters to carry a pediment that itself breaks forward twice again to enclose a great pelican bleeding in her Christian piety. Rising above, on acanthus plinths, are posturing angels and seven golden candlesticks. Two of these candles are raised on carved volutes that writhe and twist with enthusiasm and topping all is the seventh candlestick set within a swan-neck pediment. There is no livelier composition in any of Wren's city churches and the reredos testifies to the value of an unbroken tradition of design. William Edney's screen in St. Mary Redcliffe, with its fragile flutter of golden acanthus leaves blown across the spirals of an iron tree, makes the same point for the city's smiths. Even the cautious John Strahan felt free to indulge in true baroque excess when he designed, in 1726, a stone organ gallery and organ case for St. Mary Redcliffe. That survives only in a print,[9] but another gallery of 1731, an only slightly more restrained design, still stands in St. Thomas's church.

It was in 1725 that Strahan came down from the gentry-house hill tops and advertised for work in the city. For the next fifteen years, until his death late in 1741, he was able to bring elements of Scottish classicism to bear on the homely and unambitious work of the city builders. By 1725 Palladianism was becoming a force in English architecture but it is a term that has to be used with caution. Its two chief apostles to the English, Colen Campbell and James Gibbs, were both Scots like Strahan, and both, unlike Strahan, were eager proselytisers for the style. But whereas Campbell, influenced by Lord Burlington, purveyed a reserved and refined version of Palladio, Gibbs's designs emphasise a warmer, more ornate and easy aspect of the Italian's work.

16

Strahan, a sensitive but cautious architect, cannot be described as a follower of either Campbell or Gibbs. If anyone influenced him directly it was William Adam, father of the more famous Robert and a Scot who never came south of the border. Strahan certainly copied the lower fenestration of William Adam's house of 1726, The Drum, Lothian, when he designed Redland Court in 1735. But he seems to have been more attracted by Gibbs's ornate Palladian handling than by Campbell's icy correctness and he was not above borrowing details from Gibbs's *Book of Architecture*, published in 1728 to offer 'Draughts of useful and convenient Buildings and proper Ornaments'.[10] Gibbs suggested in his introduction (p. i) that these would be 'of use to such Gentlemen as might be concerned in Building, especially in the remote parts of the Country'. Stylistically speaking Bristol was still, in 1728, a very 'remote part'. Certainly the city was to remain, perhaps because of Strahan's early direction, more Gibbs than Campbell in its classicism for the rest of the century. Bath, always the rival neighbour, was, under John Wood's direction, austere and Campbellian in its Palladian work.

For this reason John Wood's references to Strahan in his *Essay towards a Description of Bath* are suspect. A Bristol deal merchant and housing speculator, John Hobbs, had employed Strahan to build houses in Bath, thereby endangering Wood's own much grander schemes. In the first 1742 edition of his *Essay* Wood claimed that Strahan 'offered his services as an architect to the citizens of Bristol, the beginning of December 1725',[11] but in subsequent editions he cut this date out: a clear sign that he had been corrected and that Strahan had been in the area much longer, at the Bishop's House in 1711 and at Cleve Hill around 1723. December 1725 was almost certainly the date when Hobbs 'took him under his Patronage'[12] and began to employ him in both cities.

Hobbs leased land in Prince Street in August 1725 and in 1726–7 Strahan built a pair of houses for him, numbers 68 and 70. A little later, after Gibbs's *Book of Architecture* had come out, Strahan built No.66, next door, for Noblett Ruddock. All three are linked by the Strahan device of the framing band of raised stone running below the cornice, but because No.66 is perhaps three years later than the others, with the Gibbs book published in between them, there is an interesting shift, not necessarily an advance, in Strahan's style as illustrated by the group.[13]

His first pair with their banded pilasters, twin pediments and segmental-headed windows are, the linking central pilaster apart, a virtual replica of the east front to Strahan's last house at Cleve Hill. This makes them the best possible proof of the influence of gentry upon urban housing in the city. To some tastes also they are Strahan's best domestic work and the most confident, because in them he handles only the elements with which he is most familiar. There is no striving after Gibbs or Vanbrugh, but the twin houses still command a length of dingy dockside road with assurance. And it is all done by recessed planes. This apparently unremarkable pair achieve their authority by a complexity of movement. Hardly one feature of their elevations is on the same level as its neighbour and the keystones of the two central windows in the rustication are a study in themselves.

By comparison, the slightly later house next door is brash, huffing and puffing with its giant order of Ionic pilasters to attract attention. Too much is going on for one three-bay facade, but its hyperactivity must have found favour because Strahan repeated the design for another client at No. 12 St. James Barton with the addition of a Gibbs surround to the door.[14] Both the surround and the stepped voussoir were taken straight from the 1728 *Book of Architecture*. They are, strictly speaking, Palladian features, but only when applied within Palladian rhythms and relationships. Bristol's contractor-builders were to pick up both the door and the window and apply them with cheerful abandon to house elevations for the rest of the century but with minimal Palladian effect.

Strahan's last work for the city was a self-contradictory duo, Redland Court of 1735 and Redland Chapel (1740–3), that exemplify all his personal indecisiveness about style. With the Court he made a real effort to produce a convincing Palladian villa with the correct bay rhythm of 1/3/1. With the Chapel, five years later, he went right back to those subtle baroque planes, frames and recessions where he was happiest. In this last he produced as a consequence his finest building.

Redland Court has not been lucky. John Cossins, the wealthy London grocer who commissioned the design from Strahan, ruined the proportions of its south front in 1747 by paying Thomas Paty to extend it by two extra bays, thus making it a 2/3/2 facade.[15] Even before that the setting of windows in its Ionic portico had been a clumsy transposition of the fenestration of an earlier house which Strahan probably designed, No. 32 College Green, now destroyed.[16] The fairest way to judge this side of the Court is to look at Strahan's 1735 design and even here it is obvious that the handling of windows brought out the worst in him. There are no fewer than ten different window surrounds on the one quite modest front. The effect is toy-like and only the grand terracing and steps down to the stalactitic gatepiers on the road pull it together.

On the north side everything is as Strahan left it, a brooding melancholy composition. He has taken his ground floor windows and door from William Adam's The Drum of 1726, but not lightened the composition, as Adam had done, by a large Venetian window on the floor above. Instead, the heavy window lintels of Strahan's upper floor over-emphasise the horizontals of a front which his usual recessed wall spaces fail to enliven.

Inside the Court is sober but direct. A Doric theme is first struck in the entrance hall with a correct triglyph frieze around the walls and a doorcase with Doric columns that leads into the reception rooms. The scale of these is almost miniature but the western staircase is the setpiece of the house with a semi-dome supported on a horseshoe-shaped Doric entablature. Round arches and recesses emerge as the dominant motif and there is none of the hesitation that mars the exterior.

Perhaps the Redland Chapel was John Strahan's most successful design because once again he was not looking over his shoulder at what someone else had done. That and the fact that for its best elevations, those to the east and west, it has virtually no windows to confuse him. With no boldly projecting columns and only a

18

single small semi-circular window high in the pediment, the entrance front to the Chapel still contrives to be neither flat nor blind. The giant order of Ionic pilasters are not even fluted and the central niche over the door holds no statue, but the ashlar surface around all these features has been shaved and incised so that the apparently solid front is alive with slight shadows and hints of depth. In contrast, the projection of the pediment is bold enough to be called Vanbrughian and pulls all the attention upwards to Strahan's unique invention of a tower-octagon-cupola-gadrooned dome. This is again something of a toy and a miniature, but so ingenious with its stone consoles which seem to be strapping the gadrooned top down against a high wind and its unglazed portholes penetrating to an interior darkness, that it all works more like sculpture than building. It is worth following the dull, unrelated side walls round to enjoy the framed recesses in the angles of the external walls of the chancel and the strange blocked and blind arch above yet more recessed shadow play on the east wall. Strahan may not have been a great architect but he was an intensely original one working out his isolated solutions to elevational problems here in the south-west, far away from the confident Scottish classicism of his youth.

Finally, the ultimate Strahan experience, literally as well as metaphorically, is the interior of the Chapel. To appreciate the theatrical functionalism of his design, it is necessary to attend a church service. There is little mysticism at the heart of Protestant worship. It is in essence communication with a central performing figure and therefore theatrical; so it was as a theatre, even to the provision of a permanent, silent audience, that Strahan conceived the place.

First there is an octagonal foyer for social intercourse. Steps lead up from this to the gallery with all the best seats: six arches in two tiers with John Cossins and his wife Martha by Rysbrack set in niches as patron saints of the chapel. The nave is plain except for the rows of serious, dimpled cherub heads carved along the guilloche frieze, all looking attentively inwards. Then comes the great proscenium arch with its Corinthian order. The baroque apsidal curve of the sanctuary is alive with Thomas Paty's highly secular carvings, and there above them, where normally there would be a window and light, is a stucco curtain being raised by an angelic hand to reveal a final painted Glory.[17]

It would be pleasing to know that Strahan lived long enough to see that final curtain rising. But from the reference in John Wood's *Essay* of 1742 to Strahan as 'lately deceased',[18] it appears that he died late in 1741 leaving his chapel in the uncertain hands of William Halfpenny. And still, with the fifth decade of the century opening, Bristol had no confident Palladian architecture, only this cerebral and old-fashioned baroque.

CHAPTER ONE - NOTES

1 The treaty, negotiated in 1703, granted differential duties favouring the importation of Portuguese wines into England to the disadvantage of the French, thus displacing the drinking of Burgundy wine by that of port.

2 John Latimer, *Annals of Bristol: Volume 2, Eighteenth Century* (Bristol, 1970), p.58.

3 For Barbon's speculative schemes see John Summerson, *Georgian London*, 2nd revised ed. (1962), pp.44-51.

4 Quoted in H. M. Colvin, *A Biographical Dictionary of British Architects 1600-1840* (1978), p. 787.

5 For Frampton see *Country Life*, 8-15 October 1927; for Cleve Hill at Downend see Rev. Emlyn Jones, *Our Parish of Mangotsfield*, reprinted ed. (Bath, 1979), James Norris Brewer, *Delineations of Gloucestershire*, 1825-7, p.169 with plate and Bristol Central Library: Loxton Drawings.

6 For Bishopsworth see A. Gomme, M. Jenner and B. Little, *Bristol: an architectural history* (1979), plate 90 on p.116. Further references to this seminal work will be given as Jenner in recognition of that writer's contribution on the 18th century.

7 Quoted in Walter Ison, *The Georgian Buildings of Bristol*, 2nd. ed. (Bath, 1978), p.153.

8 Another possible Tully house of this period which has similar articulation of window bays is the present Area Health Authority HQ in Frenchay.

9 Illustrated in Ison, figure 3, p.53.

10 James Gibbs, *A Book of Architecture Containing Designs of Buildings and Ornaments* (1728), Introduction, p.(i).

11 First, 1742 ed., Part the Second, p.17.

12 *Essay*, 1765 ed., reprinted (Bath, 1969), p.242.

13 No.66 had a twin, now demolished.

14 Illustrated in Jenner, plate 101, p.128.

15 Thomas Paty's accounts for this work are given in J. Charlton and D. M. Milton, *Redland 791 to 1800* (Bristol, 1951), appendix ii, pp.61-2.

16 Illustrated in Jenner, plate 100, p.128.

17 A pen, ink and wash drawing by James Stewart junior showing the original interior is in the British Library (K. Top. XIII 95a); a copy of this hangs on the wall in the Chapel.

18 *Essay*, 1742 ed., Part the Second, p.17.

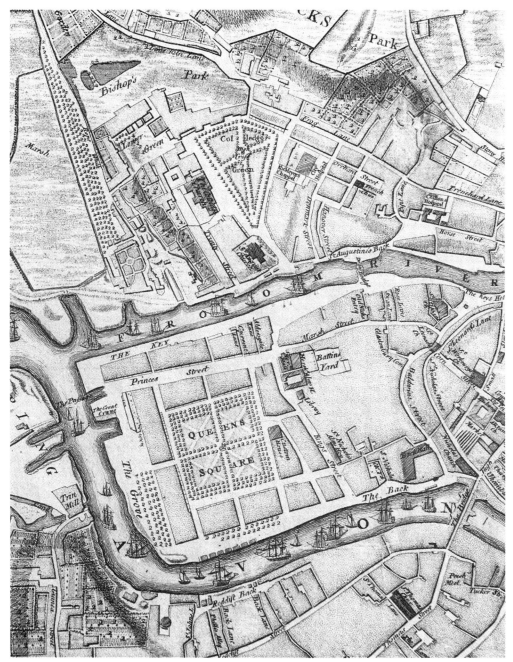

Queen Square, College Green and part of the old city centre on Rocque's Map of 1742.
(Bristol Reference Library)

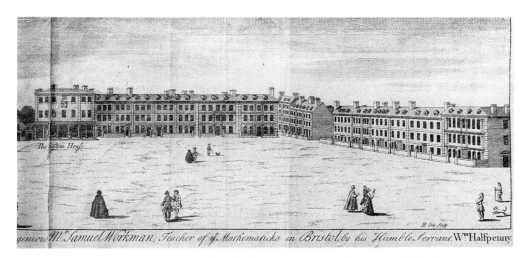

The north-east corner of Queen Square from Halfpenny's *Perspective Made Easy* of 1731. The earliest four-storey houses can be seen in the centre. (Bristol Reference Library)

29 Queen Square (1709–11) with mannerist keystones more appropriate to a much earlier house.
(Royal Commission on the Historical Monuments of England)

23

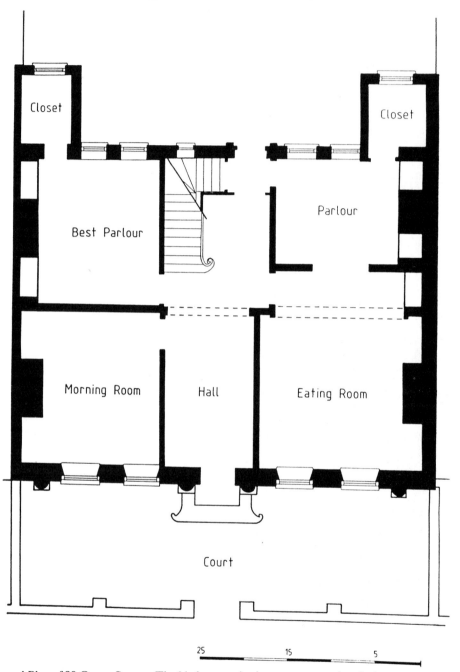

Ground Plan of 29 Queen Square. The kitchen was in the rear courtyard as the basement was used for storage of goods.

The Bishop's House, Clifton Green of 1711. A baroque emphasis on the central bay and a framing band below the cornice.

Vanbrugh's eccentric baroque on the east front of Kings Weston House (1712–14).

An early attempt to provide a pedimented central feature on the north-east side of St James's Square (1707–16); since demolished.

Orchard Street of 1718–22. Speculative building with the walls 'carried up above the Eves' as stipulated in the leases.

28 Orchard Street with its Ionic doorway and a rich newel cluster at the foot of the stairs.

Redcross Street, perhaps Bristol's first terrace and a probable George Tully design. The central house survives.

All Saints (1716–17), a brilliant resolution by George Townesend to a tower that had lost
its direction.

Protestant baroque of 1716 – the reredos at St Thomas. Paintings have replaced the Creed and the Commandments.

68 and 70 Prince Street, 1726. John Strahan's subtle play of advanced and recessed planes.

66 Prince Street – an indigestible intake of Gibbsian motifs.

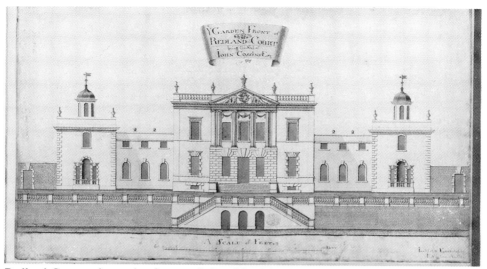

Redland Court – the garden front as designed by John Strahan in its original villa proportions.
(British Library)

The north front of Redland Court (*c.*1735) preserving Strahan's original 1/3/1
elevation.

Redland Court - ceiling in the Doric order to the main staircase.

Strahan's engaging play of recessed planes on the entrance to the Redland Chapel (1740-3).

The theatrical sanctuary of the Redland Chapel with its hand of God suggests the designing influence of William Halfpenny.

Thomas Paty carving at its superlative best in the Redland Chapel reredos. The cherubs were long believed to be Rysbrack's work.

TWO

Palladio Imposed and Palladio Improved – John Wood and William Halfpenny

The death of John Strahan was a rare lucky break for William Halfpenny in 1741, an otherwise frustrating and disappointing year. Ever since 1723, when he had offered to build Holy Trinity, Leeds with a replica of the Mausoleum of Halicarnassus instead of a spire (a device which he had characteristically filched from Nicholas Hawksmoor),[1] Halfpenny had been angling for a real commission to add a little substance to his prolific outpouring of pattern books. Leeds had fobbed him off with £1.11s.6d. Fulham had rejected outright his design for a timber bridge across the Thames. From Surrey he moved to Bristol where the Council had been procrastinating over the building of a new Corn Exchange ever since 1717. Scenting a profitable and highly prestigious commission, Halfpenny made the 'draught' of what was, by his eccentric standards, a reasonably orthodox Palladian Exchange. It was topped with something that can be best described as an onion obelisk and had two clocks, each telling a different time, but the rustication was massive and the windows were placed sparingly so it was meant to be fashionable. Halfpenny presented it to the Mayor and Council. Then, to publicize his gesture and perhaps rouse a little popular support for the design, he included it as one of the twenty-eight copperplate engravings in his fifth book, *Perspective Made Easy*, published in 1731.

Whatever the judgement on Halfpenny as an architect (and he has had few admirers) he has to be taken seriously as an architectural journalist.[2] He had a clever line on classicism made easy for the aspirant small-time builder and some of his earlier books like *Practical Architecture* went into as many as seven editions. Sometimes he reads like the confidence trickster he may well have been, but he had trained as a carpenter and that experience, combined with a genuine gift for mathematics, made him a natural bridge between lofty theory and builder's yard practice.

Bristol was a natural target for Halfpenny. It was prosperous but unsophisticated; it lacked a dominant architectural figure but was well-stocked with hopeful house-carpenters. Until Halfpenny's arrival neither Bristol nor Bath had ever had an architectural textbook explicitly aimed at them. *Perspective Made Easy* had not only the draught for an Exchange but a number of views of the two cities and a large unfolding drawing of Bristol's Queen Square. The elevation for an Exchange was slipped quietly into the Council's files and Halfpenny was still plaintively demanding payment or its return ten years later. But there is very little doubt that the publicity created by the book brought Halfpenny two rewarding commissions, one in Bath, one in Bristol.

For obvious reasons no client who actually employed Halfpenny was ever subsequently eager to record the fact. So neither Rosewell House, on Kingsmead Square in the middle of Bath, nor No.59 Queen Charlotte Street, Bristol, has ever been suggested as additions to Halfpenny's meagre oeuvre. If bad jokes are registered in Heaven, the sensitive John Strahan must still be writhing at the frequent attributions of these bizarre but lively houses to his name. It has always been accepted for stylistic reasons – the strange aprons, the excess of original ornament and the emphasis on the second floor windows – that the two houses must be by the same architect. Rosewell House is dated 1735 and No.59 Queen Charlotte Street, which began life as humble and brick-bound as its next-door neighbour, was leased in 1736 by the wealthy Jacob Elton and rebuilt. So for two years at least Halfpenny will not have gone hungry. What should have betrayed his designing hand were the bearded caryatids around a first floor window of Rosewell. These features were particular favourites of Halfpenny's pattern books. He called them 'termany' and applied them indiscriminately to his classical, Chinese or Gothick designs. Once Rosewell is accepted as Halfpenny's work he has to be given No.59 as well, merely on the unique aprons and brackets that link the upper windows of each house to its top cornice. No one else could possibly have designed such perverse features. No.59 is, nevertheless, first-rate street scenery and, with its patchwork of inter-connecting baroque oddments, is a wonderfully crazy house, worth any five of its dull neighbours. Architectural outsiders like Halfpenny throw the world of conventional design into a new perspective.

Apart from these ventures the 1730s was not Halfpenny's decade. He had taken advantage of the close commercial links between Bristol and Ireland to design a 'horse barracks' for Hillsborough[3] and in 1739 submitted two designs to the Chapter of Waterford for a new cathedral in that city: a splendid instance of his self-confidence. Either design would have made a fine nonconformist tabernacle with a schoolroom attached but Waterford was not impressed, and by 1740 Halfpenny must have begun to study the buildings that were actually going up in Bristol and started to revise his ideas. It was a time for a change of image.

The sudden rise of Bath from a squalid little wool town to an elegant spa-city had made Bristol aware, at long last, of the fashionable Palladian and of the need to catch up with the times. Frenchay Manor was just being completed on the outskirts of the city and one civic building, the City Library, was having its foundations laid in King Street. Both were more Palladian in intention than in detailed achievement, but alongside them No.59 Queen Charlotte Street must have looked distinctly odd.

Frenchay Manor is a thin house, grossly over-detailed for its small size. Into a Palladian frame of rusticated ground floor, side pavilions, piano nobile and Corinthian portico, its architect has crammed long baroque windows with raised stone panels. There is no vacant space to rest the eye. It remains, however, an undeniably eye-catching house from the roadside, conveying gentry status with the minimum expense of land or masonry, ideal therefore for a city merchant.[4]

The Library on King Street is far more relaxed as a composition. It has a pediment to stress the correct, though in this case quite inappropriate, 1/3/1 bay rhythm of a Palladian villa and Halfpenny must have been impressed by it because he copied its disproportionately dominant first floor in two of his later Bristol designs: No.40 Prince Street and the Cooper's Hall. There is, of course, a slender chance that he had controlled his disastrous ebullience and designed the Library himself, but it is usually credited to the man who carved the learned cherubs, which once sat studying on the cornices of the tall windows until a bad restoration swept them away. This carver was James Paty, an early member of that clan of builders, carvers and architects. Halfpenny will have seen Paty, George Tully and the City Surveyor, Jacob de Wilstar,[5] as his chief rivals for the prize of designing a new Exchange.

For rebuilding was in the air again and in 1739 and 1740 poor Halfpenny bombarded the Council with a marvellous variety of new designs for the Exchange. They all survive in the Bristol Record Office and should be on public display as examples of alternative design in a hidebound age.[6] Most of them are generously scattered with 'termany' figures; one seems to have copied the Elizabethan tower of Burghley House in Northamptonshire, another has a huge central rotunda set on arches. It is as if a Victorian eclectic designer had been fired back to 1740 on a time trip. Halfpenny's imagination unfortunately knew no bounds.

If they failed to impress the Council's committee for the Exchange and Markets, they may well, however, have persuaded Richard Bayly that here was the man to design a stately frontispiece for the old premises which he had bought at No.40 Prince Street. Halfpenny had been involved in a 1738 survey of the site and the five-bay elevation that was reared up in 1740–1 and brought down by bombs in 1941 had freakish touches of icicle work in its parapet and vermiculated blocks to its door columns. These were hints of Halfpenny humour and the enormous first floor windows suggest that he was making one of his magpie raids on the casual proportions of James Paty's City Library. Whatever its sources, it was a handsome elevation and plain proof that Halfpenny was, on occasions, prepared to conform. For the Exchange competition and his reputation in the city it came too late.

Halfpenny had probably always been out of his depth here. His real rivals were not locals but experienced outsiders. The Council had their eyes on architects of national standing. After idling so long in the provincial shallows, where John Romsey's directives had left the city, it was time for Bristol to rejoin the national main stream. William Jefferies, an architectural sophisticate on the Council's Exchange Committee, had acquired Isaac Ware's overwhelmingly correct Palladian design for a London Mansion House and could judge Halfpenny's efforts for the amateurism that they were. When London turned its back on Ware's design and began in 1739 to build its Mansion House to the designs of the elder George Dance, complete with an 'Egyptian Hall' in the height of Palladian fashion, Dance was invited down to Bristol and an appointment made for an interview. It was then that the unpredictable happened. Bristol, which had contentedly followed its self-chosen, rather dowdy, path of building design for decades, capitulated abruptly to a Bath architect and Bath commercial interests.

Everything happened so suddenly that there must have been a plot. On 10 December 1740 Jefferies was required by his Committee 'to go to Bath to treat with Mr. Allen or any other persons that will undertake the whole building of the Exchange'.[7] George Dance's visit was politely cancelled. John Wood of Bath was interviewed by the Committee on 6 February 1741 and asked 'to form designs'. A mere seven days later Wood laid his designs and proposals, which must have been prepared earlier, before the Committee. They were accepted on the spot and a project which had been delayed since 1717 went through in just over a week.

Ralph Allen of Prior Park, owner of the Bath stone quarries, seems to have been behind it all, wheeling and dealing. He agreed to deliver Bath stone at the Bristol quays at eleven shillings a ton, a very favourable price. But John Wood's bravura performance back in 1731, when he had saved the tower of St Nicholas's church after two Bristol builders had proved ineffectual, must have given him a high reputation in the city.[8] When the Committee went on, with the same unprecedented speed, to award contracts for the work, the most important contract, that for the fine masonry, went to a Bath man, William Biggs and his Bath free masons. His tender of £1,967.18s.9d. was temptingly set under the magic £2,000 level. The two Bristol masons who put in bids were both well over it. Thomas Paty offered to do the work for £2,312.16s.8d., James Paty offered £2,655.16s.8d.

By way of consolation to Bristol interests the rough masons' contract for laying foundations and handling unskilled rubble work went to three Bristolians: Walker, Daniel and Foot. But there was no consolation for William Halfpenny. Disappointed over the rejection of his designs, for which the Council had rewarded him with a meagre five guineas, he put in for the carpentry contract. This again went to Bristolians: Millard the younger, Samuel Jones and Samuel Glascodine on 21 April 1741. Halfpenny, resilient as ever, began to ingratiate himself with the Coopers' Company in their negotiations with the Council for compensation for their old hall, which had been pulled down to make room for the Exchange. He had to wait a year, until May 1742, before John Cossins appointed him to direct the final building stages of the Redland Chapel at a lower salary than any skilled worker on the site.

Meanwhile the Committee for the Exchange had begun to realise just what kind of a bargain they had made in appointing John Wood. A man of vision and drive, he was, perhaps inevitably, intensely self-willed and quarrelsome. Work on the new Exchange proceeded briskly but never smoothly. In March the Committee took the disastrous decision to appoint as their clerk of works and watchdog an ex-army officer, Captain Edward Foy, who had good Bristol connections but no experience of building work. Foy compensated for his ignorance by a profoundly mistrustful nature. On 3 April 1741 he begged the Committee to get a second opinion on Wood's designs from 'Lord Penbrook or Burlington Mr James or Mr

Gibbs', Wood's proposals being 'as mean and low, nay lower than ever I saw any'.[9]

Wisely Wood ignored the Captain and dealt directly with the City Chamberlain. As Wood was to be paid a 5% commission on the final costs the Committee pressed anxiously for an estimate, requests which Wood blandly refused. The case for a superior Bristolian expertise was not helped when one of the foundation arches which the rough masons were building collapsed. Soon Captain Foy was suggesting that he was in physical danger from directed masonry every time he climbed the scaffolding. One of his tap room spies reported that Biggs, the Bath mason, had boasted in his cups, 'we will have the Captain off too 'ere long'.[10]

Apprised of these threats Wood retorted that his Bath journeymen had been so intimidated in Bristol that they 'had rather starve here than go to Bristol again'.[11] But the real hidden battle was waged over whether Wood was to be allowed to build a two-storey 'Egyptian Hall' behind the Exchange. This had not been in his first proposals but Palladio had rated such Halls as an architect's pinnacle and Wood, who had been frustrated in an attempt to raise one in Bath, was desperate to achieve one at Bristol's expense. He even printed a broadsheet dated 13 July 1742 by which time any change of plans would have been almost impossible, appealing to the citizens of Bristol over the heads of their Council. This document urged that, though a two-storey open hall might be 'somewhat GLOOMY as to the Light: but then it will be *Elegant, Magnificent* and entirely *conformable to the Squares erected by the Greeks and Romans*'.[12]

The Council gritted their teeth and ignored him. In an effort to ease the awful tensions between Captain Foy and Wood they had appointed a second clerk of works, David Lewis, pointedly at a higher salary than Foy, so now they had two clerks on one building operation, one to keep the peace, the other to disturb it. In fairness to Wood it should be said that his designs, when he got round to making them, were admirably clear and precise, and the great Exchange, Bristol's most ambitious building since St. Mary Redcliffe was vaulted in the Middle Ages, was ready for its ceremonial opening on 21 September 1743, at a cost, land included, of £56,352.

John Wood's name was not mentioned in the formal speeches. Perhaps the Council had heard enough of him and thought his percentage fee of £833 was reward enough. Characteristically, Wood printed another broadsheet as a private celebration of the event. This contained a delightfully vainglorious poem written by Wood himself and entitled: '*Address'd to Sir Abraham Elton Bt. Mayor and Corporation*':

> See, see, at length the finish'd Structure rise
> A Structure that with Gresham's Labours vies!
> A stately Pile by publick Spirit plann'd
> Politely finish'd – regularly Grand
> With striking Beauties how it charms our Eyes!
> A Roman Structure gracing British Skies!
> Each Beauty blended in a fine Design

Such art Palladio – and such Jones – was thine!
And such is Wood's – who rear'd this spacious Dome
A finish'd Wonder for each Age to come.

Self praise is said to be no recommendation but Wood, who had hit drowsy Bristol like a refreshing gale from the east, had no need of it. No sooner had he given Bristol its first real Palladian design than the rival port of Liverpool was at his doorstep begging him to do the same for the north-west. This, through his son, John Wood the younger, he did, between 1748 and 1754. So Bristol could claim, in a sense, to have set an architectural fashion.

The Exchange elevation to Corn Street and the Nails is almost a hackneyed subject. Surrounded now by massive Victorian banks it is not easy to appreciate how its relaxed and confident grandeur must have altered Bristolians' awareness of their street scene. In 1744 Samuel Glascodine's rigidly orthodox Palladian gateway to the Markets added a new note of discipline to the largely medieval High Street. Even more direct in its response to the heightening demands of Wood's new Exchange was the Post Office which Glascodine was contracted to build as a right-hand pavilion to the main elevation of the Exchange on 18 April 1746. Here was the Corporation itself actually thinking in terms of Palladian design and commissioning a three-storey, three-bay 'pavilion', so formal and correct with its round-arched arcade and its pediment that the design was long credited to Wood himself. Once Bristol and its builders got an idea in their collective heads that idea was retained conservatively, and when the matching left-hand pavilion was built years later in 1782 by Thomas Paty, it copied Glascodine's outdated prototype carefully.

Wood's elevations and his basic planning deserve more than a token eulogy. What he designed at the Exchange was in an authentic west country sub-school of Palladianism. Wood may have kept a close watch on the creations of Colen Campbell and Isaac Ware, but he always saw himself as the cultural heir to Inigo Jones, hence the reference to Jones in his triumphal psalm. He used the natural exuberance of Thomas Paty's carving to achieve an unprecedented floral and fantasy richness. The frieze slung carnival-wise in permanent festival between those Corinthian capitals gave a truly Bristolian dimension to the design. Wood attempted nothing as cheerfully riotous in Bath. Bucolic in the very best sense of the word, it reflected the city's prosperity with authority and originality.

The central arch in this frontispiece leads into a vestibule of elegant shadow. Neither wholly an interior or an exterior space it works dramatically between the feminine lightness of its Corinthian order and the rigid masculine confinement of the flat ceiling bearing down on the foursquare walls. This is how Wood's lost interiors of stone at Prior Park must have looked. And it was only a prelude to the drama which the Victorian roof to the central court of the Exchange has destroyed: a sudden burst into the open air with colonnaded walls backed by ever-wilder fantasies of Paty carving, savages and strange beasts to symbolise Bristol's world trade and repeated garlands of those festive flowers. At a stroke it raised the city's aesthetic sights and converted mere merchant calculation to well-founded urban pride.

In this new climate Halfpenny began mildly to prosper. While he had presided at Redland Chapel on John Cossins' pittance, he had managed to persuade Thomas Paty to add the heads of cheerful blackamoors as bizarre label stops to the east end. Strahan would never have countenanced such popular excess but Halfpenny's pattern books brim with it and Paty would have been in the mood as he was carving turbanned warriors down at the Exchange in just these years, 1742–43. But Halfpenny's real reward and the proof of his adaptability to the aesthetic climate of an environment was the series of relatively authentic Palladian buildings which he was able to build in the city in the wake of John Wood's resounding demonstration piece.

No.40 had already added a slightly eccentric Palladian dignity to Prince Street. Now, between 1743 and 1744, came Halfpenny's Coopers' Hall in King Street and then, in 1746, Clifton Court up on the villa-scattered slopes of Clifton Hill. The Assembly Rooms on Prince Street would be his last incorrect but lively offering to the city in 1755, the year of his death. At some point in his last ten years he must, on stylistic evidence alone, have designed a bizarre masterpiece in the Black Castle at Arno's Court, but that, being Gothick, belongs to the next chapter.

Self-confidence was both Halfpenny's strength and his weakness. He not only believed that the great Palladio had made many mistakes, but that William Halfpenny was the man to correct him. In 1751, primed by his recent Bristol experience, he published a book with the misleading title of *Andrea Palladio's First Book of Architecture*, 'wherein is pointed out the various Mistakes and Contradictions between the Chapters and Figur'd Draughts; laid down both Geometrical, and in Perspective, in an entirely new and easy Method'.[14] In this he aired his home-brewed insights with the usual twenty-eight copperplate engravings.

Within limits his Coopers' Hall and his Clifton Court (now the Chesterfield Nursing Home) justify his impertinence. Both buildings succeed by a defiant insistence on that trick he had learnt from the City Library: a disproportionately lofty first floor. Coopers' Hall may be all wrong in its proportions but it emerges as most effective street scenery and the visual core of King Street. Its squat, rusticated ground floor and underplayed entrance seem to stagger under the weight of the enormous Corinthian portico and the giant windows. Halfpenny was making a Palladian feature behave more like a baroque giant order. There is no place here for delicacy and the balustrades above and below are all blind. On top of it all sits an over-wide pediment and an attic storey that seems to have come from a completely different building.

Clifton Court is more subtle; the polite surroundings of Clifton Green have exercised a moderating influence. But again, within Palladian limits, so much is going on. The quoining changes its mind when it reaches the broad platband and switches from the banded to the rusticated. In the half-rusticated ground floor there are segmental-headed windows inset just like those in No.40 Prince Street.

Above them the first floor windows tower up on baroque panels to further recessed panels that have been cut to keep any potentially vacant wall space busily active. As a final defiant roughness, the side walls have been faced with the grim black clinker from the city's brass foundries.

It is a particular sadness that Halfpenny's last building, the Assembly Rooms on Prince Street, should have been lost as it spanned three stylistic phases of Bristol's classical development. The money for the Rooms was raised in 1754 by a tontine and they were completed in 1755 to mark Bristolians' acceptance of a new and elegant order to their social life as the Exchange marked with its tavern, coffee-house and open forum, their commercial dealings. Eclectic to the last, Halfpenny designed a pediment that was baroque in its lively backward break and Palladian in its ugly, undersized windows. Its third element was Rococo even, in its enchantingly odd ballroom, a Chinese Rococo.

This last style had already made a very tentative first appearance in Bristol at Clifton Hill House, Isaac Ware's villa of 1746–50 which belongs more properly to the next chapter. It was Ware's plasterer, Joseph Thomas, who applied to the walls of the ballroom a slightly more animated version of the stucco patterning that he had laid on the ceilings in Clifton Hill House. Rocaille and acanthus swirled about the clock on its west wall and the topmost quarterpieces twisted above the central arched feature like dragons' tails are what Ware describes as 'wild leaves.'[15] From a basket of grapes and two masks, garlands of fruit and flowers tumble down about the Chinese Rococo mirror, which was, it must be admitted, the only authentic Chinoiserie in the room.

Balls were held on alternate Thursdays in winter. Minuets began sedately at half-past six, the more roistering country dances from eight o'clock until eleven when the Master of Ceremonies closed proceedings. A subscription of two guineas allowed entry for one citizen with two ladies, provided that the ladies wore hats. An organ and an orchestra provided the music.

The inscription in letters of lead over the entrance to this civic night spot should be read as William Halfpenny's epitaph: CURAS CITHARA TOLLIT, Music dispels Care. He died, in debt predictably, but still writing confidently about Chinese architecture, on the strength, no doubt, of his travels in Ireland.

CHAPTER TWO - NOTES

1   The design is illustrated in Halfpenny's *Art of Sound Building* (1725); Hawksmoor's church inspired by the Mausoleum of Halicarnassus is St. George, Bloomsbury (1716–31).

2   For Halfpenny's journalistic career see Eileen Harris, *British Architectural Writers 1556–1785* (Cambridge, 1990), pp.218–28.

3   The barracks were designed in 1732 for the 1st Viscount Hillsborough.

4   The house was built after 1736 for a wealthy Quaker merchant, Joseph Beck.

5   John Jacob de Wilstar acted as Surveyor for the Corporation and had prepared a plan for the Exchange which was under consideration in June 1740.

6   Bristol Record Office, 04713 and 1024 (1–16); some are illustrated in Ison, plate 15.

7   Bristol Record Office, Minutes of the Committee for Building the Exchange and Markets, 19 December 1740. A definitive account of the construction, citing all relevant sources, is given in Tim Mowl and Brian Earnshaw, *John Wood: Architect of Obsession* (Bath, 1988), Chapter 10 (pp.149–68). Subsequent references to the building of the Exchange will be made to this Chapter.

8   Latimer, 2, pp.179–80.

9   Mowl-Earnshaw, p.154.

10 Ibid., p.155.

11 Ibid., p.155.

12 Ibid., p.156.

13 Ibid., p.161.

14 Title page.

15 Isaac Ware, *A Complete Body of Architecture* (1756), p. 525.

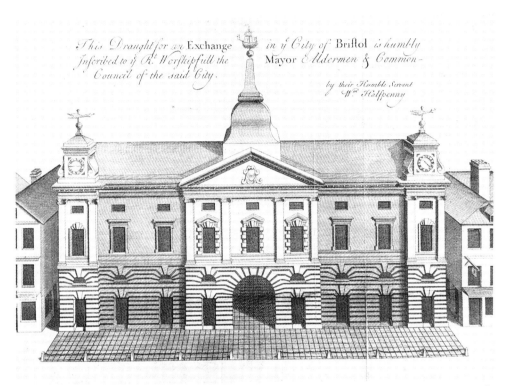

Halfpenny's first bid to build the new Exchange, a relatively sober design of 1731 from his *Perspective Made Easy*. (Bristol Reference Library)

59 Queen Charlotte Street (1736). Halfpenny's hyperactive refronting of a plain brick façade like that surviving on the right.

Halfpenny's bizarre Rosewell House of 1735 – an exuberant riposte to the sobriety of Bath.

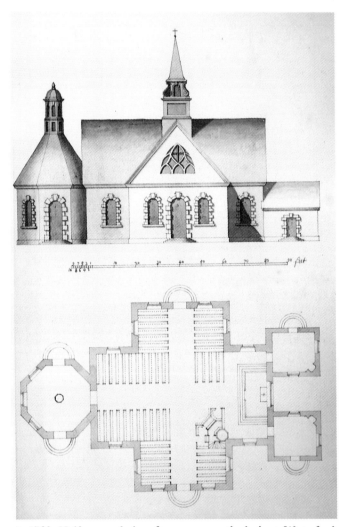

A 1739 Halfpenny design for a new cathedral at Waterford.
(British Architectural Library RIBA)

Over-panelled Palladian or flattened baroque? Frenchay Manor of 1736, a merchant's cheap passport to gentry status.

40 Prince Street (1740–1) destroyed in the Blitz. A Halfpenny design with disproportionately tall first floor.

The Corn Exchange of 1741-3 – John Wood's correct Palladian elevation softened and enriched by Thomas Paty's figurative frieze.

Pure, stony Palladianism in the vestibule of the Exchange.

Bucolic Rococo – Thomas Paty's Asia panel with camels and gryphons in the Exchange.

Blackamoors' heads on the east end of Redland Chapel, a Halfpenny gesture carved by Thomas Paty on a Strahan recessed plane.

Coopers' Hall (1743-4). William Halfpenny's dramatically successful rough handling of the Palladian.

Clifton Court of *c*.1745 – elongated, un-Palladian proportions and return walls faced in black industrial slag.

The Assembly Rooms (1754-5) on Prince Street, demolished 1956. A baroque pediment over undersized Palladian fenestration.

Prince Street Assembly Rooms – Joseph Thomas's plasterwork familiarised Bristolians with Rococo design.

THREE

Gothick and Rococo – The City's Paradoxical Duo

Some architects, Isaac Ware among them, tended to treat the Rococo more as a disease than a style. It is ironic, therefore, that Ware, who was an almost morbidly fanatical Palladian with a deep mistrust for 'French decorations', should inadvertently have introduced polite Bristol to the suspect French delights of Rococo design. This seems to have happened when he was building that desperately pure Palladian villa, Clifton Hill House, on the last vacant ledge of the cluttered slope around Clifton's old church. The house was for a rich merchant, Paul Fisher, and it went up between 1746 and 1750 at just the time when 'French decorations' or, as the French themselves referred to it, the 'genre pittoresque' ('Rococo' is a much later term), was infiltrating England from the Continent.

The Rococo was a highly unusual style in that it had a most distinctive interior profile, instantly recognisable with its sinuous asymmetrics, but never developed a generally accepted exterior form. This will explain why architects tended to treat it with suspicion. Their usual reaction in this country was to compensate for the self-indulgent intricacies of interior plasterwork by ruthlessly austere exteriors of classical ashlar, relieved by the occasional canted bay. Sir Robert Taylor led the way in these odd manifestations of Protestant guilt.[1] As a result the Rococo remained an essentially decorative style with great appeal only to craftsmen as it allowed them riotous opportunities to demonstrate their skills in plaster, wood or metal. And because Bristol in the 18th century rarely escaped from the craftsmen-turned-builder to proper professional architects, it meant that the city responded far more openly to the Rococo than it had ever done to rule-laden Palladian with all its obscure, elitist snobberies of harmonious proportion and correct ornament. In the Royal Fort the city produced from its native resources of skill what is certainly a masterpiece and arguably the most complete and enchanting Rococo house in Britain.

But the Fort was for the future; it was built between 1758 and 1760. Back in 1746 at Clifton Hill House the balance between architect and craftsman was still uncertain. Paul Fisher paid Thomas Paty £2,000 to realise the chilly serenity of Isaac Ware's designs, and decades later when Paty was designing houses for himself on Great George Street and elsewhere he had still not recovered from the icy restraints that this earlier experience laid upon him. Joseph Thomas, who was paid £406 for his plaster work in the house, seems to have found the experience less inhibiting.

There is an intriguing near-certainty that Thomas had already decorated his own modest house, 5 Guinea Street, with a fine ceiling of a far more committed Rococo design than anything Ware allowed him to raise in Clifton Hill House. Thomas had negotiated the leases for the Guinea Street property on 5 September

1740 and that usually implied that the house or houses would be built within the next two years. His ceiling had the central feature of C-scrolls and rocaille decoration with asymmetrical panels in the corners of raffle leaves supporting squirrels and birds.[2] These last were characteristic of the 1740s. One of the delightful features of Rococo art was that along with all its abstract twirls and curlicues, it could be overtly figurative. Palladian classicism had dammed up the natural human instinct to copy the real world; now, taking their inspiration from obscure trade pattern books like Matthias Lock's *Six Sconces* (1744) and *Six Tables* (1746), craftsmen like Thomas could scatter grinning Chinamen, fork-tailed dragons, ho-ho birds, squirrels, goats, foxes and dogs liberally over the intricacies of panels that wilfully defied symmetry and balance. Essentially the Rococo was a protest movement and, since John Romsey's ill-conceived decrees of 1699, Bristol craftsmen had more to protest against than most.

Isaac Ware must have been proud of Clifton Hill House because he included a plate of it in his *A Complete Body of Architecture*, published in 1756.[3] It was the most reserved and minimalist of all the major elevations that he illustrated and the only one in which the windows are cut straight into the ashlar without architraves. The text of the book is revealing. Recalling the pressure to which clients like Paul Fisher and Lord Chesterfield had subjected him, he wrote that sometimes 'the fancy of the Proprietor, we readily allow, must be satisfied at the expense of this rigid propriety'.[4] Joseph Thomas's three setpiece ceilings for the house, over the stairwell and in the dining and drawing rooms, are closely related to plates 74 and 83 in Ware's book. Ware was an admirer of Inigo Jones's ceiling designs and he has kept Thomas confined within the firm bounds of geometrical compartments in the fashion of the 17th century. Inside these, however, there has been some, reluctant, permissiveness. There are no actual squirrels, goats or ho-ho birds craning down their long necks, but Ware did accept figurative devices which he believed, with ponderously fake scholarship, to have some historical precedent: 'those grotesque representations of the human form which we received from the Moors and Arabs, boys or virgins to the waist and from thence terminating in scrolls wound about with a wild freedom'.[5] Sigmund Freud would have enjoyed himself if he could have had Isaac Ware on his couch. Thomas also took advantage of Ware's allowance that 'upon the head of a figure may be a basket of fruit or flowers'.[6] Diana and Ceres both perform this balancing act over Fisher's dining table and the fruit basket was to remain a staple of Bristol's Rococo design throughout the period. Thomas would establish it on the polite mind by featuring it prominently about four years later in his decorative work for the Assembly Rooms.

What does not feature at Clifton Hill House is the characteristic Rococo motif of 'a ceiling straggled over with arched lines, and twisted curves, with X and C's and tangled semicircles'. These, Ware declared, 'may please the light eye of the French who seldom carry their observation farther than a casual glance'.[7] Instead Joseph Thomas was allowed to hyperventilate his acanthus scrolls until they approximated to the true Rococo 'raffle' leaves or 'wild leaves' as Ware nervously describes them.

Also, to be fair to him, Ware did urge his craftsman that 'the flowers of our own country, with those raised by the curious in their gardens, will give him a choice of a thousand varieties, or let him turn to the *British Herbal* and the *Body of Gardening*'.[8] This was revolutionary advice from an arch-conservative and may well have inspired the freshness and accuracy of Bristol's best stucco work. Nothing in the city's Rococo design was ever to be as tightly formalised again as the Clifton Hill House ceilings, but in the shell and acanthus sunburst over its stairs and the dog-headed scrolls and basket-bearing goddesses of its dining room there is a fertile tension working between two opposed generations of decorative thinking. It is the frozen Spring before the Royal Fort's warm Summer.

The usual arid complexities of unresolved, and probably unresolvable, attribution must be faced now, as briefly as possible, because they are unproductive. Craftsmen like Joseph Thomas are naturally less literate than architects. They leave few records. They worked in teams. They altered their styles to meet the whims of their paymasters, the clients. As a result they often left brilliant work to which a name can only be affixed by the lucky break of a recorded payment or the tempting but unreliable game of stylistic analysis. Obviously an architectural historian loves the solid ground of a name to brandish, and over the years it has become customary in the south-west to apply the name of Thomas Stocking to any plaster decoration of a lively nature and reasonable artistic quality made between the 1750s and the 1770s. Yet in 1775, Sketchley's *Directory* listed no fewer than twenty-seven tylers and plasterers active in Bristol alone.

Real certainties about Stocking are rare. He died in 1808, aged eighty-six, leaving his property to his wife Mary. Before that he had fathered a son, also Thomas, who had become his apprentice in 1765, probably at the age of fourteen. Stocking is only known with certainty to have worked at Stoke Park House with the Patys between 1760 and 1764, at Corsham Court, where he was paid a substantial £710 for work between 1763 and 1766, at Fonmon Castle in Glamorgan where he worked with the Patys and received minor payments in 1766-7, and at St. Nicholas's church by Bristol Bridge, where around 1768-9 he devised the whole vast ceiling, working again alongside the Patys.[9] In the 1790s he was sharing a house at 16 College Street with a carpenter and a baker. A romantic notion is current that he came over from Ireland around 1760. There is nothing to support this, but he is unlikely to have been a Bristol native as he only became a free burgess, on payment of a fine, in 1763, when he was already forty-one.

All the other attributions to him of plasterwork at Hagley Hall, Worcestershire (*c*.1758), Arno's Court (1756-8), the Royal Fort (1759-60), Frenchay House (*c*.1771), all in or near Bristol, and at Beacon House, Painswick, Gloucestershire (*c*.1767-9), can provide the useful bones for a biography, but they are no more than intelligent guesswork.[10] Joseph Thomas, who began so early, lived on until 1777, but his dull Welsh surname has not caught the historians' fancy. Stocking sounds like a wild and lively Irish lad. Associate his name with the dazzling, poetic and undoubtedly 'wild' plasterwork on the staircase at the Royal Fort and it is easy then to go on brazenly and attribute the wild and rather ridiculous hop garlands on the Boudoir dome of Kyre Court, Worcestershire of about 1776 to Thomas Stocking.[11]

Achievements must weigh more heavily than names. After Thomas's Assembly Rooms of 1754-5 had advertised the Rococo to the rich citizens at their fortnightly winter balls, the next work, on stylistic evidence, is that on the stairs and dining room of Arno's Court, dating from perhaps 1756-8.

Psychologically rather than aesthetically the buildings of Arno's Court - the house, the stables, the arch and the bath house - are more interesting even than the Royal Fort. Thomas Tyndall who had the Fort built between 1758 and 1760 knew his own mind; he revelled in the human graces of the Rococo and continued to patronise the style even when, at the rebuilding of his own parish church of Christ Church, it was phasing into the neo-Classical. William Reeve, the pugnacious, extrovert, Quaker copper smelter and brass founder who ordered the Arno's Vale buildings into existence, was anything but stylistically single-minded. In Reeve's artistic patronage the whole fascinating dualism of mid-century Bristol is encapsulated. On the one hand is the Gothick, essentially at this stage an exterior form, ferocious in its profile, threatening, patriotic and historicist. On the other lies the Rococo, internal, decorative, sybaritic even, alien and unpatriotic in its Gallic associations. And Reeve bestrode them both before, with a drama more proper to his Gothick than to his Rococo psyche, his fortunes crashed into humiliating bankruptcy.

An almost Jonsonian symbolism attaches to the two men, as if their careers had prepared them both for parts in *Volpone*. Tyndall, living high in his gracious, airy villa on the hill, was rich but kept his hands, if not his soul, clean on the proceeds of the triangular trade in African slaves to America. Reeve was also rich but his hands and possibly his lungs must often have been very dirty. He had settled in Brislington in the old buildings of Arno's Court, low down in Arno's Vale close to his mills and foundries. These last poured out their toxic fumes and soot in the narrow confines of the Avon valley at Crew's Hole. Environmentally, Reeve was a disaster, but he kept a large workforce profitably employed, as environmental disasters tend to do.

Thomas Tyndall's grandfather, Onesiphorous, founder of the Tyndall fortunes, had been a nonconformist, but Thomas had settled into the comfortable arms of the Established Church. William Reeve was a self-made, 'where there's muck there's [literally] brass' man, and he was still a Quaker. He had, however, challenged a barrister who ridiculed him publicly in a law suit to a duel with swords, pistols or fists, and wrung an apology from him. In the best story-book tradition, that barrister later became Lord Chancellor and treated Reeve to a dinner of reconciliation. No more is known about Reeve except that his fortunes probably peaked in 1765 when he was Master of the Merchants Society. In 1774 he went bankrupt. Arno's Court in its revised Gothick dress and the Black Castle were 'lately built' when Horace Walpole passed them on 22 October 1766 with one of his usual, spiteful references to any Gothick work that rivalled his own Strawberry Hill.[12] This accords with the date, 1764, on one of the Castle's pinnacles.

At some unrecorded date Reeve added a complete classical villa, which he called Mount Pleasant, to the rambling buildings of the old Arno's Court. In its first form this villa had the characteristic self-denying exterior austerity of a house with a Rococo interior: two narrow, canted bays facing the road from Bath. Only two Rococo rooms have survived. Whoever designed their ceilings had come to grips with a problem that was still exercising Isaac Ware in 1756: what happens when the rigid, old-fashioned compartments that had been imposed at Clifton Hill House are abandoned? Ware's conclusion was to consider the whole ceiling as one great panel. The 'forward and backward C's in which the French so much delight' could be used as a loose but serviceable substitute for the more correct geometry of designs by Inigo Jones:

> the hollows made by these curvilinear figures at the sides and corners may be easily and agreeably filled up with ornaments, and in this manner may be formed the division of this ceiling, which although a work of fancy will not shock the eye by any glaring impropriety, and will be agreeable with all its singularity.[13]

These are the words of a wise conservative in retreat, and this is exactly the advice that the plasterer followed over the stairs at Arno's Court. Light frills of rocaille, raffle leaves and old-fashioned nosegays describe a sprightly oval around a timid centrepiece. The drawing room ceiling is more daring. There pheasants are flying among great trails of naturalistic roses and peaches. Also the ho-ho birds are in flight, their sinuous necks bent to peer down at the family. Here, at last, is a real Rococo ceiling, yet it still retains a slender but quite unnecessary curvilinear compartment, so it has not quite escaped those geometrical shackles that Ware wanted to retain.

The two interesting and related problems about the Arno's Vale complex are: who designed the extraordinary Black Castle, and what was the sequence of the Gothick and the classical work?

Anyone who reads that the Black Castle, a building Walpole scornfully dismissed as 'the devil's cathedral',[14] is merely the stables and offices to the Court, should pay the site a visit. The Castle is the size of a considerable country house. Four tall towers are set about a large court of one and two-storey buildings and the complex is dominated by an even taller gatehouse and keep. This last contains a 'Chapel' with a barrel-vaulted ceiling formed into panels by richly decorated mouldings. Underneath the 'Chapel' was a large hall converted now into a public bar, but through gaps in the suspended ceiling can be seen grotesque faces apparently supporting a vaulted roof.[15] Obviously the Castle was designed to be something more than a mere stable block. It was the administrative centre for William Reeve's substantial industrial enterprises, but the interior decoration indicates that Reeve used it as a suite for entertaining and pleasure.

The classical front and reception rooms of the present Arno's Court may have been added to the original old Court buildings as Reeve's foundries prospered and only later he indulged himself in the eccentricity of the Castle. For eccentric it certainly is, being composed of the light, but iron-hard black slag from the Quaker's brass foundries. Even today the visual impact of this material is demonic. Its windows, doors, ornaments, battlemented parapet and string courses are all in pale freestone which makes a dramatic contrast but renders the whole slightly unreal, like a child's dreadful toy.

It is perhaps the baleful impact of the slag which has distracted observers from the ambitious nature of the Black Castle's design. Just for once this seems to be an 18th century Bristol building which cannot possibly have been designed by any of the Paty clan though it was almost certainly constructed by them. There is an outrageous boldness, also a crudity, to this shock of towers and turrets that smacks of William Halfpenny's later pattern books. *Chinese and Gothic Architecture Properly Ornamented* came out as late as 1752 and was produced jointly with John Halfpenny, the son who survived him. The ogee gables on the two flanking walls of the courtyard both have recessed panels of a curious double ogee which Halfpenny often used in his designs. These appear again on the gateway which originally stood in the forecourt of the Castle and now stands isolated and a little lost alongside the main road. Another detail on the gateway, half strapwork and half Gothick tracery, features on one of Halfpenny's designs for a cathedral at Waterford.

Most tellingly, both the interior court of the Castle and the gateway carry sets of the caryatid pilasters that Halfpenny called 'termany'; not that they terminated anything, but as has been noted at Rosewell House in Bath, they were a curious feature of his designs. A whole row of them is set with arms akimbo across the inside courts of two of his failed 1739–40 designs for the Exchange. No other 18th century designer is ever recorded as using them as a standard decorative device.[16]

Stylistic comparisons never make final proofs, but there has to be a strong likelihood that one or other of the Halfpennys designed the Black Castle for the brash, newly-rich Quaker industrialist. Reeve built it when the classical addition to Arno's Court proved inadequate for his entertaining. Reeve subsequently updated the plain, pinched bays of the Court. Examination of the stonework reveals that all the Paty-designed Gothick detail of the windows and the porch has been added later.

The Bath House stood roughly half-way between the Castle and the Court. It was an original Paty design with no hint of Halfpenny, its colonnade is close to one that James Paty devised in 1763 to make a new north porch for Stoke Park House. Before it was allowed to decay and be carted off by Clough Williams-Ellis to decorate his complex at Portmeirion, this unique building served as a stylistic link between the Castle and the Court. Its overall classical appearance was paradoxically conveyed by an orderly disposition of Batty Langley-style Gothick features: arches, columns, capitals and ogee domes. Here William Reeve's binary attraction towards two opposed but psychologically complementary styles came harmoniously together. Its siting has been questioned, but to anyone with the imaginative reach to recreate the years when Bristol was the industrial Black Country of Britain, it was ideally sited and perfectly functional. In those days, thrusting foundry owners were not afraid of grime and grease. When they supervised their workers they got dirty. Driven back to his stables around the Black Castle after a day in the foundry, the first need of Quaker Reeve would have been a bath. And there, half-way between his stables and the Court, was his Bath House with ante room, dressing room and plunge pool for industrial hygiene as well as for pleasure. The pool chamber was a long octagon lit by two octagonal roof lanterns. Its plasterwork was Chinese Rococo in mood like that of the stairs at the Royal Fort. Dolphins, fountains, shells and water gods created a decor of informal charm. A tunnel cut under the road gave Reeve private access to his house.

A plausible sequence for the Arno's Court buildings would run as follows:

1740   William Reeve settles in the old Court

c.1756–8   An architect unknown, possibly James Bridges, designs the new villa in a plain classical style

c.1763–4   The Black Castle and its gateway is built by the Patys to a Halfpenny design

c.1764   The Patys design and build the Bath House

1765   The Patys add a Gothick trim to the classical villa

In reviving the memory of a complex where such separate aesthetic moods had been brought together it is useful to remember what a strange city Bristol was in that middle century, bristling with mediaeval towers, black with active collieries in the new suburbs, filthy with foundry smoke, its rivers then as be-slimed and muddy as they are today. Alexander Pope described it in 1739 as 'very unpleasant, and no civilised company in it. The streets are as crowded as London; but the best image I can give you of it is, 'tis as if Wapping and Southwark were ten times bigger'.[17] To Horace Walpole it was 'the dirtiest great shop I ever saw'.[18] Reeve's Black Castle was the dark Gothick response to its smoke, its engines and its industrial turmoil. Thomas Tyndall's Royal Fort was the Rococo escape from it all. The Rococo-Gothick Bath House was the rational compromise between the two.

What also needs to be noted is that Bristol was Chatterton's city. Thomas Chatterton, 'the marvellous boy', appears less marvellous if he is seen as the natural product of an environment where Arno's Vale was just down the road from his 1752 birthplace. His poems are the precise Bristolian mid-century mix of Gothick and Rococo strivings. He tends to be remembered for his pastiche of 15th century poetry, 'As wroten bie the gode priest, Thomas Rowleie', every bit as clumsy and boldly unconvincing as the Black Castle and Halfpenny's Gothick taste. But he also wrote quantities of bland pastoral verse in the Rococo vein of that other side to contemporary Bristol. Vapid eclogues like:

Lucy since the knot was tied
Which confirmed thee Strephon's bride,
All is pleasure, all is joy,
Married love can never cloy.

> Learn, ye rovers, learn from this,
> Marriage is the road to bliss.[19]

are in sharp contrast to the Gothick overdrive of:

> His long sharp spear, his spreading shield is gone,
> He falls, and falling, rolleth thousands down.
> War, gore faced War, by Envy armed, arist,
> His fiery helm nodding to the air,
> Ten bloody arrows in his straining fist.[20]

It was this easy movement between conflicting emotional moods that made Chatterton appealing to Bristol patrons. Nonconformity can breed tensions to which it offers no religious release. Hence those Quaker ladies of the Goldney family toiling for almost thirty years, from 1737 onwards, to create their grotto: a place of calculated gloom yet alive with the glitter of spa and quartz crystals, with a lions' den for Daniel and pagan Neptune commanding the flow of waters. The same obscure drive led William Champion, another Quaker and copper smelter, to raise his own private Eblis, a black, clinker grotto in the garden of Warmley House, Kingswood, and to set up a monstrous, twenty-foot high idol, the Warmley Giant, to glare back vacantly towards the conventional classical facade of his house.[21] It was only when Quaker William Reeve had gone bankrupt that the Society of Friends expelled him with the mealy mouthed reproach: 'it appears the conduct of William Reeve hath been reproachful and inconsistent with our religious principles'.[22]

Chatterton's associates were lesser men of the same breed, the foolish bibliomaniac George Catcot, James Thistlethwaite with his 'literary tastes' and Lambert the attorney who employed Chatterton until the boy faked a suicide note and alarmed him. These were the provincial intelligentsia of a rich, squalid yet romantic industrial city, the Pittsburgh of its day. They responded easily to the dual register of Chatterton's poetry, the fake and the effete, the Gothick and the Rococo, because of their Bristol background. Born into such a society and such a city it was quite natural for Chatterton to fake translations of Saxon poetry and to draw his own Halfpenny-style world of crude, bold Saxon churches and fake Norman castles.

When Chatterton was one year old, Norborne Berkeley, Bristol's local squire of Stoke Park House, a man with twelve uninterrupted generations of male succession behind him and some very profitable collieries at Stapleton, began deliberately to fake a large, towered Jacobean house literally on top of his existing, genuine but small, 16th century manor. Before Chatterton's brief seventeen-and-a-half year span was over, the pliant Patys would have built a Gothick gazebo tower for the Quaker owner of Goldney House, then bewilderingly surrounded it with a classical loggia.[23] Cote House on Durdham Down would have been raised in Gothick shape as wild and improbable, with its pinnacles, its battery of ogee windows and its fake screen walls, as anything that the Black Castle had attempted.[24] Stoke Bishop Manor almost next door to Cote would have been ogee-windowed over in emulation. Still in that short lifetime St. Werburgh's and St. Nicholas's churches within the city walls would have been rebuilt by James Bridges in a mediaeval dress so convincing that they were actually dull.[25] Then Blaise Castle would have gone up on its wooded hill-top in elegantly trefoiled Gothick form[26] and finally, Norborne Berkeley, having revived the bogus title of Baron Botetourt in his own favour, would have changed his stylistic mind and decorated several rooms of his new-old Jacobean castle in the contemporary Rococo style.[27] This was the directional confusion to which poor Chatterton and his seedy coterie of antiquaries and bookshop browsers responded. A cheerful falseness was in the air, Bristol was a nouveau riche society with all that that implies in unfettered enthusiasm and undirected taste, vulgarity but also achievement.

What then, in all this stylistic uncertainty and these architectural exercises of doubtful value, produced the Royal Fort? The answer is as unexpected as it is unsatisfactory as it is true. The Royal Fort was a Paty team effort. Because they were a firm of builders rather than one commanding designing figure, the Patys were able to put together brilliant, and the word is used advisedly, carvers of wood and stone and at least two superb craftsmen in plaster, one an erratic poet of the realised visual image, the other a masterly formalist. With all these men working easily together, with the house relatively small and the money supply unstinted, only an architect for the outward elevations was missing and even that came right on the day.

Behind that pliant, biddable collection of talents there must have been the positive force of a single-minded and sophisticated client. Thomas Tyndall, third generation rich, was one of the rare Bristol merchant-gentry who knew what he wanted. If the decorative themes of the Fort are any guide he was fond of shooting, fishing, pretty girls and possibly music. He was prepared to put his money into one stylistic movement, the Rococo, at exactly the time in the Seven Years War (1756–63), when French fashions were most unpopular and the Anti-Gallican league was flourishing. It was a Bristol mob that had chanted in 1754:

> No general Naturalisation! No French bottle makers! No lowering of wages of
> Working Men to 4d. a day and Garlick![28]

when it was proposed that a few Huguenots should be offered British citizenship. Tyndall seems to have enjoyed the garlick flavour. His firmness of purpose was rewarded by a complex and provoking artistic unity.

Instead of commissioning one elevation to define the house, Tyndall hedged his bets and built three of equal importance. Each can be read as a separate essay on the mid-century theme of 'Whither Palladio?' The result is a house that demands to be walked around and seen at angles. One proof of its success is that no two critics respond to it in the same way. Everyone appears to favour a different elevation for an unpredictable variety of reasons. Here, for what it is worth, is a personal reaction.

The north or entrance front is surly but makes sense as a preparation for the related but richer architectural experience of the hall within. The west front is a definitive Palladian statement. It is how a front should be put together to produce something conventional and bland. In fact, viewed as a single unit from the steep lawns below, it looks isolated without supporting wings. Then comes the south front and this, for me, is the most rewarding, no longer a provincial building but instead a subtle anticipation of Sir Robert Taylor's Chute Lodge, Wiltshire of *c*.1768 and his Sharpham House, Devon of *c*.1770.[29] Its canted bay is generously broad in its angles, three softly modelled female heads are set in its first floor keystones and rusticated masonry laps over carelessly on either side onto the flanking bays. Two matching doors with Rococo scrolls and heraldry give a garden openness to it all.

James Bridges is usually credited with these elevations. A contemporary poem flattering Thomas Tyndall hints at a more exotic but perfectly credible authorship:

> For Aid, – he, Jones, – Palladio, – Vanbrugh viewed;
> Or Wallis, – Bridges, – Patty's Plans pursued;
> No Matter which, – the Fabric soon uprose,
> And all its various Beauties did disclose.[30]

Three disparate elevations and three listed Bristol architects may be a coincidence; but the poem and the almost complete difference in the window architraves of the three facades suggest that Tyndall commissioned a design from each architect then paid Bridges to make a model (which survives in the house) and tie them convincingly together by unifying platband and sill-course. That would explain the odd shortening of the Venetian windows on the south front.

A hitherto unpublished letter from a later Tyndall to his uncle, preserved in the Scottish Record Office,[31] proves that, whoever was responsible for the initial exterior design, the Paty team 'did all the mason's work for the house' just as they had done at Clifton Hill House. They also handled the interior woodwork and plasterwork, being paid '30 guineas each' for the superb Eating and Drawing Room ceilings, £24 for the amazing door in the eating room and £17.10s. for the wooden trophies flanking its chimney-piece.

What actually impelled the team of skilled but hitherto cautious craftsmen into interior design of such poetry may have been Thomas Tyndall himself, or it may have been his wife, Alicia, ten years his junior, who sadly died only four years after their enchanting house was completed. The florid but basically Gibbsian rectangular designs which the Patys had carefully drawn up for the Tyndalls were rejected out of hand.[32] Instead the Patys were projected into brilliant improvisations on Chinese wallpapers and pattern books like *The Modern Builder's Assistant* which appeared in 1757 and Thomas Johnson's *One Hundred and Fifty New Designs*, published in 1758, the year the Fort was begun.[33] It was as if a modern house were to be fitted up on illustrations in *House and Garden* and some Sanderson wallpaper patterns. Not an improbable scenario and certainly a feminine one. The result was a sense of fun and domestic happiness that is still palpable in the main rooms.

What does strike a masculine note is the entrance hall with its three arches and their Doric pilasters. The Fort never loses a firm sense of spatial direction and controlled surprises. At the arches the axis switches left through shadow and under Doric friezes of military triumph appropriate to the years of Pitt the Elder. Then light pours in from the right and the intoxicating detail of climbing vines sweeps up the staircase wall with a freedom and an invention quite alien to the classical spirit of disciplined order. Foxes peer up at birds, butterflies flap, floating islands of rocaille work support goats, Chinamen and crumbling castles.

It is a received gospel now that this is the work of the wild Irish boy, Thomas Stocking. Yet the large ceilings which he is known to have created for Stoke Park House three years later, because he appears in the accounts there, are formal compositions, competent, with fruit baskets which Isaac Ware would have approved, but with no hint of these half-told stories from a willow-pattern land. His cornice of heads at Corsham Court is skilful but rigidly confined, while his vast ceiling for St. Nicholas's church in Bristol was mere curlicues and vacant spaces.

It was the directing hand of the Tyndalls that made the difference. Although the ceiling rosette above the stairwell has all the standard, uninspired, Paty garlands of leaves and roses, the superb wooden trophies of the chase on the Eating Room walls are brilliantly observed naturalistic carvings. The Eating Room doorframe, derivative of Thomas Johnson as it may be, rises like an arc of defiance and twining innovation against the staid conventions of the average Georgian decor. No one suggests Stocking carved it. Thomas Paty carved it and was paid for it, but it is in the same spirit as the plasterwork on the staircase walls because the same inspired patrons directed both.

When Alicia Tyndall died in 1764 whatever may have been intended for the first floor rooms was never carried out. The Fort did inspire one imitation down in the city. At No.15 Orchard Street an unknown plasterer, Joseph Thomas perhaps or any one of those twenty-seven listed in the directory, has pressed Thomas Johnson's designs into service again and laid a series of Chinoiserie panels up the staircase of John Worsley's house of 1722. Again the result is sheer visual escapism. Mandarins and wood demons smile and scowl. Dragons with forked tails steal peaches from a twining tree. There are peacocks, eagles, hounds' heads at the end of scrolls, Prince of Wales feathers; all turning a commonplace enclosure into shallow vistas of fantastic incident. It was no accident that those Corinthian columns flanking the Eating Room door up at the Fort were set deliberately askew. At heart the whole Rococo movement in decorative art was subversive. It was revolutionary and it had to be subdued.

Robert Adam achieved that subjection. The Gothick he could not control but he diverted the Rococo into the delicate order of neo-Classicism, complex but formal. That figurative invention which made Rococo plasterwork so rewarding was lost in the colour and precision work of Adam ceilings. Rococo plasterwork was rarely delicately moulded. It relied not on colour but on the shadow thrown by bold relief, hence its detail as at No.15 Orchard Street is quite coarse, semi-sculptural. By 1771, when Thomas Homfray was employing the inevitable Patys to decorate his

Frenchay House, they had fallen back to their well-tried old favourites, those garlands of heavy roses that had not altered since the 1730s.[34]

There was just to be one last and unexpected flowering of the Rococo in Bristol, and once more Thomas Tyndall seems to have been its inspiration. Christ Church in the city centre was his parish church and he was, by his wealth, a highly influential parishioner. So when it was rebuilt between 1786 and 1790 by young William Paty, fresh from architectural training in London, it can hardly have been chance that the new church was modelled on an interior created in 1765–8 by Sir Robert Taylor, the leading architect of the English Rococo. This model was not another church (Gibbs's St. Martin in the Fields is often cited), but Taylor's Transfer Offices at the Bank of England. If labels serve any purpose Christ Church has to be described as neo-Classical by its date though Rococo-Classical in its essence. It must, therefore, be reserved, reluctantly, to its chronological place in the next chapter, the only city church to match the Royal Fort in spatial daring and in decorative lightness of spirit.

CHAPTER THREE – NOTES

1   For Taylor see Marius Binney, *Sir Robert Taylor: From Rococo to Neo-Classicism* (1984).
2   A line drawing of this plasterwork is given in Ison, title page; text on p.47.
3   Plate 40.
4   Ware, p.522.
5   Ibid., p.498.
6   Ibid., p.498.
7   Ibid., p.522.
8   Ibid., p.500.
9   For Stocking at Stoke Park: Gloucester Record Office, Badminton Muniments, D2700; Corsham Court: Frederick J. Ladd, *Architects at Corsham Court* (Bradford-on-Avon, 1978), appendix D; Fonmon Castle: Glamorgan Record Office, Fonmon Archives, 11/50/5 (I owe this information to Sir Brooke Boothby); St Nicholas Church: Ison, pp.65–70 and Jenner, plate 139. Stocking was also paid £5.15s. in 1781 for unspecified work at the Theatre Royal in Bristol (B.R.O. 8978 (3): Account Book 1).
10   Attributions to Stocking at Hagley: Christopher Hussey, *English Country Houses: Early Georgian 1715–1760* (1955), p.198 and plate 355; Arno's Court: Nikolaus Pevsner, *The Buildings of England: North Somerset and Bristol* (1958), p.363 (giving William Stocking); Royal Fort: Jenner, p.174; Frenchay House: Department of the Environment List of Buildings of Special Architectural or Historic Interest; Beacon House: David Verey, *The Buildings of England: Gloucestershire 1 The Cotswolds* (1970), p.363 (giving William Stocking).
11   Hussey, p.221 and plate 396.
12   *Horace Walpole's Correspondence*, ed. by W. S. Lewis, volume 10 (Montagu II 1762–1770), p.232.
13   Ware, p.524.
14   Lewis, volume 10, p.232.
15   The former Great Hall of the Black Castle is illustrated in A. E. Tilling, *Guide to Arno's Castle*, no date.
16   The two Exchange designs in the B.R.O. are: 1024(11) and 1024(16); the latter is illustrated in Ison, plate 15.
17   Quoted in Latimer, 2, 223.
18   Lewis, volume 10, p.232.
19   From 'The Happy Pair'.

20   From 'Chorus from Goddwyn'.

21   William Champion set up his Warmley works in 1749 for the production of zinc on a commercial scale, using ore mined on the Mendips. The giant Neptune stands between a canal and an eyecatcher-boathouse and is bordered by a caravan park; see Barbara Jones, *Follies & Grottoes*, 2nd revised ed. (1974), pp. 212-13.

22   Quoted in Sheena Stoddard, *Mr. Braikenridge's Brislington* (Bristol, 1981), p.42.

23   The original form of the gazebo is shown in a sketch of 1788 by S. H. Grimm, illustrated in P. K. Stembridge, *Goldney A House And A Family* (Bristol, 1969), pp.14-15.

24   Cote House was probably Gothicised about 1759 for William Phelps. There is an early watercolour of the house by J. M. W. Turner (*c.*1792) in the collection of the Cecil Higgins Art Gallery in Bedford. See also Brewer who includes a plate.

25   For St. Nicholas see Jenner, pp.171-74. The tower and spire were completed by Thomas Paty between 1764 and 1769 after James Bridges had left Bristol disillusioned. Paty's steeple is impressive in scale with a bold profile but its detail is an unscholarly Gothick.

26   The sham castle was designed for the merchant Thomas Farr in 1765 by Robert Mylne who was currently working at Kings Weston. Farr built it in 1766.

27   James Paty was contracted to supervise the second (1760-4) phase of building in conformity with Thomas Wright's designs (Badminton Muniments, Gloucester Record Office).

28   Quoted in *Rococo: Art and Design in Hogarth's England* (Victoria & Albert Museum Exhibition Catalogue, 1984), p.15.

29   Binney, plates 42 and 43 respectively.

30   Written pseudonymously by J. W. Shirehampton (Ison gives John Wallis) and quoted in Ison, p.190.

31   From T. O. Tyndall to Onesiphorous Tyndall Bruce (S.R.O. GD 152/53/6/9/7). Cited and quoted with the approval of the Keeper of the Records of Scotland.

32   A series of ten designs for the interiors of two rooms, attributed to Thomas Paty were auctioned at Christie's in 1982. One was acquired by the City of Bristol Museum and Art Gallery (illustrated in the V & A *Rococo* catalogue, M20 on p.206), another by the University of Bristol. I am grateful to Francis Greenacre, Curator, Fine Art of the City Museum and Art Gallery for making available his collection's drawing for scrutiny and to M. J. H. Liversidge of the University for his insights into the series of designs. The interiors have certain affinities with the Royal Fort but cannot with certainty be connected to the house.

33   Whereas Paty's woodcarvings are inspired by Johnson, the decorative plasterwork closely resembles designs by Timothy Lightoler in *The Modern Builder's Assistant*. Plate 80, a ceiling design with central eagle, is particularly close to that in the Eating Room.

34   The Paty authorship of Frenchay House is a stylistic attribution based on the similarity of the canted bay treatment there and at the Royal Fort, and on the drawing room cornice which is identical to one on the Paty drawing now owned by the City Museum and Art Gallery.

Clifton Hill House (1746–50) built to Isaac Ware's frigid design by Thomas Paty and a model for later Paty housing. (Bristol University Department of History of Art)

A ceiling panel by Joseph Thomas at Clifton Hill House edging towards Rococo forms via Isaac Ware's approved mannerist motifs.

The Rococo-classical villa addition to Arno's Court (*c.* 1756–8) with its Gothick trim of 1765.

Probably the first flight of Thomas Stocking's pheasants and ho-ho birds on the Drawing Room ceiling at Arno's Court.

The keep and inner court of the Black Castle, a William Halfpenny design realised by the Patys shortly after his death, and the Bath House at Arno's Court – a James Paty design of *c.*1764 that encapsulated the moment of Gothick and Rococo interaction. The façade now re-erected at Portmeirion. (City Museum and Art Gallery)

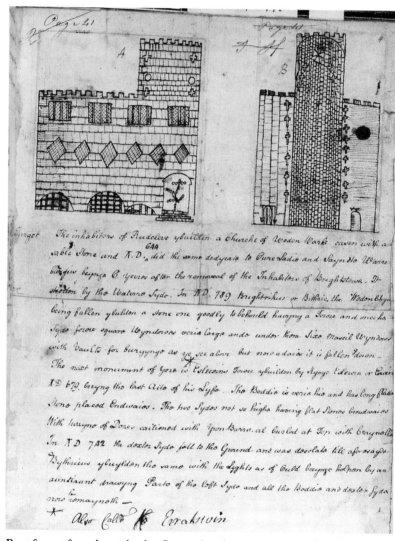

Page from a forger's notebook – Saxon churches and the Dark Age chronicles of Bristol as invented by Thomas Chatterton. (British Library)

The Grotto at Goldney House created 1737–64 by Quaker ladies. Neptune and Daniel's lions confuse the allegory.

'Thou shalt not make any graven image' – the Warmley Giant, a garden
ornament cloaked in brass clinker for Quaker Champion.

Stoke Park House (1749–63) – Thomas Wright's fake Jacobean castle built for Norborne Berkeley by the Patys.

Walls to the bastion garden at Goldney House and the Gothick garden temple originally enclosed in a classical colonnade.

Cote House – rebuilt in 1759, painted by Turner in the 1790s and demolished in the 1920s. A lost prodigy of Bristol Gothick preserved in this Loxton drawing. (Bristol Reference Library)

Palladian design moves from left to right into Rococo under Thomas Tyndall's sophisticated patronage at the Royal Fort (1758–61).

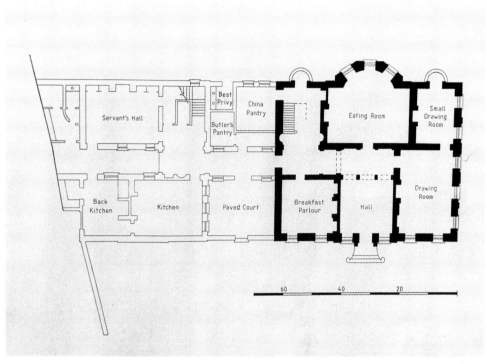

A ground plan of the Royal Fort – a Rococo villa added to an earlier house which then acted as its service area.

Royal Fort, hall archway and staircase – both spatially and decoratively the most poetic Rococo interior in Britain. (Bristol University Department of History of Art)

Royal Fort, the Eating Room furnished without furniture by Thomas Paty's doorframe and trophies and Stocking's ceiling.

Royal Fort, Eating
Room. This sporting
trophy by Thomas Paty
surpasses, in the delicate
restraint of its
composition, anything
by Grinling Gibbons.
(Bristol University
Department of History
of Art

Royal Fort, an airy elegance of ho-ho birds and raffle leaves by Thomas Stocking in the Drawing Room.
(Bristol University Department of History of Art)

Peaches, peach blossom and a Chinese head with rocaille decoration on an asymmetrical panel at 15 Orchard Street.

The Rococo in retreat – a ceiling of 1771 at Frenchay House where the Patys have fallen back on their well-tried roses.

FOUR

The City under the Patys

Mediocrity can be as potent a factor as genius in the development of a city. It was Bristol's bad luck to be dominated between 1760 and 1789 by the two brothers, Thomas and James Paty. It was a time of moderate prosperity when many new streets were laid out and old ones rebuilt, but all in a style so conservative and unadventurous that when Berkeley Crescent went up shortly after 1787, its elevations would have seemed perfectly familiar to Queen Anne if she had been alive to view them. As a result Bristol lost for a time the sense of visual adventure and identity that makes an urban area coherent. In 1760 Clifton had still been a polite suburb. By the early 19th century its architectural initiatives had given it a centrifugal social pull of its own, and the centre of gravity for shopping and social activity had come to rest somewhere between the two rival entities of Bristol and Clifton, at the top of Park Street.

Beside the complexities of the Paty, Patty or Patey family's genealogy even the plot of *A Midsummer Night's Dream* appears simple. Not only were individual members unable to fix on a constant spelling of their own surname (one actually changed it in the course of writing his will), but even its pronunciation seems to have varied. As a further complication they favoured the Christian name James to confusing effect.

The Patys were a clan rather than a single family, one of masons and carvers. There were at least two branches: one, the Pattys (with variant spellings) had their building premises in the Horsefair, the other, the Patys (also with variant spellings) had a large building yard in Limekiln Lane behind College Green. It was to this latter branch that the important Patys, who exercised a generally stultifying influence on the city's architecture, belonged.

First came the two brothers, sons inevitably of James, a carver and mason, who died in 1747. Thomas (1713–89) was the elder, James his brother, was seventeen years younger but died ten years before him in 1779. Thomas's son William (1758–1800) was the only Paty to be properly trained as an architect in the Royal Academy schools, though both his father and his uncle styled themselves as architects on occasion and often acted as such. William joined the family firm in 1777 and worked thereafter modestly to update its building style. All three Patys were expert carvers and statuaries. Thomas was technically brilliant, particularly in wood; he was not, however, an innovative or creative artist in the real sense. Two fine pieces of woodcarving, inevitably attributed to Grinling Gibbons, which had ended up in the City Library and at Goldney House, remained a model and inspiration to him throughout his career.[1] As an architect he was equally unimaginative and conservative, devoted to brick despite being a stone carver. His idea of an elevation was to apply a few obvious features: blocked Gibbsian surrounds to doors, and windows with the tiresome and irresolute flutter of five-stepped voussoirs as a constant over each and every window. The Bristol lesene dividing all houses absolved him and his imitators from any invention of vertical features on an elevation, while horizontal elements were restricted to a conventional cornice. The result was a bland, brick box with some colour relief in freestone elements mass-produced at the Paty yard.

St. Michael's church, the body of which Thomas Paty rebuilt between 1775 and 1777 reveals how inept was his spatial handling: an illiterate compromise between the classical and the barely Gothic. His brother James, on the other hand, could produce satisfying Gothick buildings in the old-fashioned manner of Batty Langley. It was James, not Thomas, who carried through the massive works of the second stage (1760-4) at Stoke Park House. What was, however, the most complex construction work of this period, the building of the Theatre Royal (1764-66), was carried through for a fee of £200 by Thomas.[2] The Proprietors had bought a plan and section of a theatre from Mr. Saunderson, the carpenter of Drury Lane Theatre, for £38.16s.8d. This was redrawn and adapted by Thomas Paty who then supervised the entire building process.[3]

Between 1762 and 1768 there was a surge of construction and reconstruction in and around the old city and 1762 seems to have been the decisive year for the two Patys. This was the time when they broke away from their old pattern of carving and the supervision of other men's building projects to design whole streets themselves. In that one year houses to their design were going up at the junction of Great George Street and the, as yet, largely houseless Park Street, at Albemarle Row in the Hotwells and on the south-west side of King Square. But it was now that they fell into a pattern of provincial adequacy that was to infect large sectors of the city, Dolphin Street, Clare Street, Marsh Street and Brunswick Square, with a decent but uninspiring tedium of brick. Bridge Street in stone was the exception that has been lost, like so much of this building of the 1760s, in the bombing of 1941 and 1942.

Park Street was not to be continued on the lines that the Paty brothers had obviously intended by their houses at the Great George Street junction. But the 1760s expansion of the Hotwells was shaped by the pattern of modest unambitious brick that Thomas Paty imposed in Albemarle Row. Here the fault was one of basic planning and substructure. Until 1787, when his son William had become a dominant figure in the firm, Thomas rarely designed houses on an expensive foundation of cellars that had levelled a site. A terrace that slides in irregular steps down a slope ceases to be a terrace and becomes merely a handsome row of houses. This is what happened at Albemarle. Either that street should have been replanned to follow the contours, or a massive substructure should have been raised as a preliminary to any piecemeal development. John Wood and the Bath architects who followed him based the great set piece terraces of that city on level foundations. But Thomas Paty was not an architect, though named as such in the lease of No.5 Albemarle Row; he was an economically-minded, unambitious journeyman builder, who happened also to be a great craftsman. Significantly in that lease his only stated function was to finance in part the common sewer.[4] The secret of bringing unity to a row of houses lies in the financing of the land and in the binding phrases of a lease. Thomas Paty had no apparent interest in such processes.

As a result the Row descends the hill in seven steps. Two of the original houses have only three bays, four have five, the central house has seven, breaking forward under a pediment emphasised by alternate quoining. Some doors have Gibbs surrounds, some do not. It is the Queen Square story all over again. A spa like the Hotwells needed a bold and imaginative architectural treatment far more than its parent city. It had a warm saline spring inconveniently sited below the muddy high tide mark of the Avon and it had the visual drama of St. Vincent's Rocks. Until Albemarle Row was built its only real architectural asset was George Tully's minuscule Dowry Square. As Alexander Pope had written in 1739, 'there is no living at the Wells without more conveniences in the winter', although he had praised 'several pretty lodging houses open to the river'.[5]

Mineral springs were two-a-penny, a spa survived by its sense of style and Albemarle Row simply failed to satisfy that sense. Its immediate successors from 1763 onwards can be seen along Dowry Parade. First came three five-bay houses in direct imitation of Albemarle. These were soon divided shoddily into semi-detached pairs. Then the line of brick houses continues with smaller units until it falters at an incomplete house. At that point Paradise Row, a far more modest stucco terrace, takes over, running down, not to some fine structure commanding the river, but to The Rose of Denmark public house. It is like watching a candle guttering out as aspirations fade and the tone of the place is lowered.

If the Hotwells could have kept up appearances Clifton might never have risen so successfully to challenge Bristol's separate identity. But as the Hotwells sank in gentle architectural decline, its social image sank also. It remained cheap, relaxed and just a little sleazy. In 1777 visiting gentlemen 'of the true *ton*' were expressing their '*ton*' by going to drink the waters wearing nightcaps and two fob watches.[6]

High up above on its Downs, Clifton was still without a spa and had only the attractions of its superior air. The Patys seem actually to have slowed down its growth in 1763 by designing Boyce's Building for Thomas Boyce, a wig maker, in the wrong place, away from the best views, and in the wrong style: the usual old-fashioned confection of brick with a naive profusion of Gibbs surrounds in stone. It was a true terrace, built on the level with a small central pediment and curious pattern of bay recessions (3/2/1/3/1/2/3). Mr. Boyce went bankrupt in 1772 and his new lodging houses were auctioned off. It is perhaps unfair to blame the Patys for this development as no direct connection has ever been proven, but they were certainly responsible for Prospect House, built three years later on Clifton Green with its very similar show of Gibbs surrounds.

Back in the city the Paty influence was equally commonplace. At King Square exactly the same mistakes were made and at the same time as those of Albemarle Row. The Bristol tradition of stressing the individual ownership of a house by lesenes was not conducive to grand and united designs. In 1766 the development of Cumberland Street and the west side of Brunswick Square, both laid out by, though not built by, George Tully, provided a telling vignette of what happened when the Patys were not around to direct the average small-time Bristol builders. In Cumberland Street, overshadowed now by the brutal cliff of Avon House North, Thomas and Isaac Manley have obviously pleased themselves. Some modest shops have large Venetian windows on both the upper storeys, others retreat to stepped voussoirs, at least two have canted bays on the ground floor. All in all the street is an engaging illiteracy with never a dull moment. But as soon as Cumberland Street turns the corner into the new Brunswick Square the Manleys, who were still doing the building, became respectable by Paty standards and plastered their three houses with the spotted-dick effect of Gibbs surrounds as in Boyce's Buildings, only here the windows have retained their original proportions.

The south and main side of Brunswick Square was built between 1766 and 1771 by Edmund Workman. It suffered such a drastic restoration in the 1980s that it seems now fairer to attribute it to the present city planners, but at best it was never more than a revision of Boyce's Buildings, chopped vertically by lesenes and with the inevitable blocked Gibbs surrounds to the doorways.

It was in 1770 that the Paty brothers were given their real opportunity to demonstrate vision. George Tully, a veteran of Queen Square and the surveyor who had, since then, laid out most of Bristol's new streets, died in that year and the Patys succeeded him naturally as the city's favoured surveyors. But, in fact, 1770 actually marked the beginning of a lull in building activity. If it was the time for vision then that vision was wanting.

Rocque's map of 1742 shows Bristol's prime site for housing, the King's Down, as already laid out with roads from Somerset Street down to and including King Square. That was where splendid terraces and crescents could and should have risen to boost the city's image for affluence, taste and civic spirit. But the only orderly project to be carried through, a tame enough affair, was King Square. Throughout the 1770s and the early 1780s a pleasant straggle of random building invested this strategic hillside, directly above the city centre.

Wearisome and uninspired set piece achievements like Brunswick Square and Albemarle Row tend unfairly to monopolise most accounts of Bristolian expansion in this period. The reality was that far more work was being carried on in those haphazard streets on Kingsdown by small building firms such as the Manleys. There lies the real Bristol of these dull decades. It is harder to categorise such developments and civic authorities have, over the years, found them easier to demolish, but it is engaging sectors of architectural free-for-all such as Somerset Street and that fascinating first stretch of Ashley Road, from number 10 to 63 on the left after leaving Stokes Croft, that reward attention the more.

Both these streets, or half streets, demonstrate that the usual process was for a small builder to lease enough land for two, three or even four houses, two being the norm. They would then build quickly with an eye to the taste and pocket of a few likely clients, make a fast sale to cover costs and move on to the next enterprise. A fair aesthetic reaction to such developments is not easy to make. They often have great charm but rarely represent an original vision because so much has been added to them over the years. On Somerset Street for instance, almost half the houses have the stepped Paty voussoirs but at Ashley House an owner has very understandably tired of this trite effect, squashed two Paty facades into one house and added a delightfully grandiose Doric porch which was then made to carry two storeys of round bay windows. No.18 and no.19 share three Venetian windows with another house, down Spring Hill, while bay windows with margin glazing and upper windows that flaunt no fewer than nine steps to their voussoirs all compose perfectly well on the one elevation in the general higgledy-piggledy of the street. Often the shared rustication of a ground floor, as in no.12 and no.13, is the only remaining sign that a pair was built together. One result of all these casual additions is that the taller rear elevations of the houses are as architecturally impressive and chaotic as their street fronts.

That was not the case on Ashley Road. Those houses all stand behind long front gardens which were entered originally by solid rustic gates. But at their rear they back immediately onto a narrow service street without even the convenience of a small area. Squalid to the rear, but with flowery diversity to the fore, they are a most likeable set of buildings. No.25 has beautiful brickwork and a tight, elegant central bow up its entire facade. No.29 next door is a grand, ashlar-fronted house with much rustication. One builder's group is composed of numbers 17, 19 and 21: low, with balconies in romantic decay. Next to them is a taller group of five: 10, 11, 12, 13 and 14, probably by the same builders aiming at a different income bracket. Bristol is fortunately still a city for such discoveries, there are similar scatterings out towards Old Market and on Stokes Croft. They are the rewards of a city that mistrusted planning, excluded outside architects and went its own easy-going way to its ultimate detriment.

The building mania that began around 1784 and crashed so disastrously when the Revolutionary War broke out in 1793 was by no means restricted to Bristol, but in the city the mood of feckless optimism and over-construction does seem to have run unusually strongly. Visitors in the early years of the 19th century comment in amazement at the spectacle of street upon street of hollow, uncompleted houses. The most extravagant excesses of this period, and the most imaginative, took place in Clifton. But in Bristol itself, the young William Paty, who had been working alongside his father Thomas ever since his return from London training in 1777, was able to use the new mood of enthusiasm and change to direct the city into stone-building and a cautious stylistic advance. So much of what he built has been commercialised over the years that it is not easy to appreciate his original concepts. James Malcolm visited Bristol in 1807, and in his book, *First Impressions*, published that year, he described:

> a magnificent street, of white stone, unfinished, uninhabited, desolate, and almost in ruins; the houses of which consist of rustic basements, handsome

cornices, and Doric doors. The ascent is an angle of very many degrees, and the lines of the houses and their copings form complete steps.

Linked to this 'grand view' was 'a mansion of the purest white, and of the Doric order, buried in dark foliage, on the summit of a beautiful slope', with 'a lawn, descending from the front, planted at intervals, grouped with an imitation of one of the ruined towers of a castle'.[7]

This idyllic composition, like a scene painted by Claude or Poussin, is in fact an account of Park Street as William Paty originally conceived it, leading up not to the crushing bulk of the Wills Tower, but to the Royal Fort with its Rococo-Palladian facades set in a grove of elms. The precise style of Park Street, Berkeley Square and Charlotte Street is not easy to define. William Paty was influenced by Sir Robert Taylor and by Robert Adam, neither of whom had grasped the full potential of a neo-Classical exterior, so the elevations of Bristol in the great building boom are best described as late Palladian, delicately refined.

At the top of Park Street there is fascinating evidence of the stylistic battle fought out between father Thomas and son William in the years after 1787. The old man had intended to crown the hill with a grand, brick crescent but his son demonstrated that a three-sided square would make a more economical use of the ground. His father seems to have staged a General Custer's last stand for conservative brick against the light stone ashlar that had crept up the hill, and what was actually built is a strange compromise. The entrance to William's Berkeley Square of stone is guarded by Berkeley Crescent in Thomas's old style brick raised upon a highly expensive substructure. Across the road the north side of Berkeley Square presents an even odder image of dualism. The elevations into the square are of William's polite stone classicism, a slightly more expensive version of the Park Street stepped houses. But its outer face, almost hidden now by the clutter of shops on Queen's Road, is faced in Thomas's old-fashioned brick and stone with not a detail spared; and it was this face that was clearly, but quite illogically, intended to dominate the hilltop. Inside the Square William had demonstrated his inexperience with a delightfully ham-fisted centre-piece, now the Berkeley Square Hotel. This has a guilloche frieze dodging under pilasters and Prince of Wales feather capitals supporting a furtive little pediment. Hyperactive indecision is written all over this façade. A scholarly three-dimensional neo-Classical feature would have pulled the whole square together, but these almost two-dimensional scribbles of carved detail go hardly noticed. Just down the hill the elevations of Charlotte Street need their ironwork balconies because their stone facades offer no feature or centring. In Great George Street, a series of detached Paty houses, by Thomas at the bottom of the hill, by William farther up, are all caught in a chaste, nervous reserve, trapped in a stylistic calm, waiting for the Greek Revival which William, in his London years, failed to absorb.

Christ Church, built between 1786 and 1790, was William Paty's undoubted masterpiece. The Transfer Offices of the Bank of England, on which it is so closely modelled, were built by Sir Robert Taylor in 1765-8,[8] so in the usual Bristol fashion it was out-dated before its foundations were laid, but it is easily the city's finest classical church. St. Nicholas, by James Bridges of 1762–9, was spatially inept, St. Michael's, by Thomas Paty (1774–7) lacked even the redeeming plasterwork of St. Nicholas. St. Thomas's, rebuilt by James Allen between 1791 and 1793, was no more than an honest container for excellent earlier woodwork. Christ Church, in contrast, has an interior of an amazing airy lightness. Every column appears to be standing on tip-toe, straining up in the effort to tether the white and gold billow of its shallow vaults to the earth. Not only are these columns very tall and slim, but perched on each Corinthian capital is a slim block of entablature. It is this frail prop, so precariously balanced, that actually sends the ribs driving out to carry pendentives and saucer domes over the wide nave. Lit up at night, the impression of space barely controlled is breathtaking, but because William Paty shirked Taylor's structurally ambitious top-lighting from domed lanterns, the interior works less well in daylight. The capitals, carved with the favourite Paty rose, should be re-gilded and the columns repainted to imitate Sienese marble as Paty decorated them. It would then convey that same sense of light-hearted worldliness that the Royal Fort exudes and draw every visitor to the city to appreciate its achievement.

Christ Church has virtually no exterior elevations, only its over-subtle tower that starts, stops, then starts again in an effort to act as both an immediate ornament to Broad Street and to be viewed effectively from a distance. Its contemporary, the Unitarians' Lewin's Mead Chapel, built between 1788 and 1791, has in contrast the lean, elegant exterior of an Adam-style ballroom. Within, Bristol's richest congregation were content with a tour de force of engineering: a 70 by 40 foot ceiling suspended high above the galleries by iron chains from timber roof beams. Unusually, the architect was a London man, William Blackburn, better known for designing seventeen prisons, all within the period when the Chapel was being built. Joseph Glascodine, the local builder, had to be content with providing the internal fittings, some of which survive the Chapel's conversion to business premises.

The drab reign of brick in the city was not quite ended. An unknown architect working to a tight budget was adding an east range to Brunswick Square between 1784 and 1786. Its slight end pavilions were an innovation but it is hard to enthuse over an elevation with such shallow recessions carrying a repetitive eighteen-bay expanse. Even the Gibbsian surrounds which punctuate the other two sides of the square had now been pared away.

Daniel Hague's Portland Square marks an even more decisive move towards London fashions here at the north-east side of the city than William Paty's Park Street out on the west. What is, however, typically Bristolian, is that among the long horizontals of its houses, built to Hague's original modish designs over an extended period (1790–1822) stands the brilliant vertical of St. Paul's church, also by Hague and begun just before the houses in 1789, but which stylistically would have been considered a trifle old-fashioned if it had been put up in 1750 by poor William Halfpenny.

St. Paul's has never been given its due as street scenery. It rears up like a defiant Gothick-Chinese pagoda providing an essential vertical marker in an area of otherwise unrelieved horizontals. Hague used all Halfpenny's tricks of recessed panels to give surface texture and large quatrefoils between the upper and lower windows. So far this was only a repeat of what he had designed a year before in the Hope Chapel above Dowry Square,[9] but now he added a vibrant tension of acute angles and lean, blocked windows to all the usual coy ogees of the Gothick. His little side porches are temples in themselves and, while there is never a dull moment, there are a number of moments of real grace. Only the interior of St. Paul's is a disappointment. For his proportions, the junction of columns and ceiling, Hague has gone to the worst possible model: Thomas Paty's dreadful St. Michael's, and not all the froth of stucco-work can distract the eye from the barn-like emptiness of it all.

The elevations of the square are richer than contemporary William Paty buildings, but to see Hague at his ingenious best it is necessary to go out again along the Ashley Road to Ashley Place where the rustication, the handling of the keystones and the sill-band betray his designing style on one of the most experimental and satisfying terraces in Bristol. Four houses with his plain pilaster strips and light modillion cornice, as at Portland Square, are linked together only on their ground, or as Bristol called it, 'parlour' floor, by a rusticated base with a mansard attic. The profile is dramatic and the composition unified, though the idea of linking basically separate houses is illogical.

Built around 1788 it must have caught the eye of Charles Melsom, a Bristol surveyor who had been casting around for a way to bring variety and order to the vacant eastern end of Kingsdown Parade, an awkward, narrow, elongated area to the east of a street of random development. Catching the last wave of hopeful investment capital that had been generated over in Clifton, Melsom persuaded a consortium of backers, that included the usual rich widow, to put money into a project for nineteen houses in a semi-detached version of Hague's Ashley Place design on the north side and twenty-one gloomy Thomas Paty-type houses on the south. This St. James's Place or St. James's Parade, the name varies, was begun in 1791 and relates oddly to other developments in the city by being in brick with only dressings of freestone. The semi-detached terrace stands back behind long front gardens with a service road immediately to the rear, consequently the whole Place/Parade never quite coheres. Later additions have dramatically confused the lively rhythms of the north terrace, but enough survives to show that, by the early 1790s, other suburbs of the city were beginning to respond to challenge and invention. The long blight of noncomformist 'conformity' was coming to an end, but too late for the city to recapture the architectural initiative from its Clifton village rival.

CHAPTER FOUR – NOTES

1   For these woodcarvings see Jenner, plates 92 and 93.

2   Bristol Record Office 8978(3): Theatre Royal Account Book 1 (1764–1914). This records the payment to 'Thos. Paty' in 1769.

3   The minutes of the Proprietors' meetings (B.R.O. 8978(1) a) record on 3 December 1764 that 'At this Meeting were produced an Elevation Ground Plan and Section of a Theatre Drawn by Mr Saunders [sic] Carpenter of Drury Lane Play House'. Saunderson was paid for this on 4 June 1766 (B.R.O. 8978(3)). The minutes further record, on 25 October 1764, that the 'Building be Immediately sett about under the Direction of Mr. Thos. Patty'.

4   Ison, p.199.

5   Latimer, 2, p.223.

6   Quoted by Latimer, 2, p.429, taken from *Felix Farley's Journal* of May 1777.

7   Malcolm, p.192.

8   Binney, plate 11.

9   The Hope Chapel was opened in 1788. Hague's authorship is a stylistic attribution based on the identical patterning of panelled pilaster buttresses in each building.

Neither lesenes nor a battery of stepped voussoirs are able to convert Albemarle Row (1762–3) from a row of fine houses into a unified terrace.

Coarsely detailed five-bay houses of 1763 converted into semis when Dowry Parade began its social decline after 1790.

Ill-sited and ill-treated – the battered remnant of Boyce's Buildings, a Gibbsian terrace, originally three houses, by the Patys of 1763.

Hit-and-miss builders' classicism by the Manley Brothers in Cumberland Street (1766).

When in doubt try a Gibbsian surround. Houses of 1767 by the Manleys on the south side of Brunswick Square.

A confusion of levels and an uncertainty of styles in the Kingsdown speculative development of 1787 at Somerset Street.

Thomas Paty's stepped voussoirs and brick on a return elevation to William Paty's stone-faced Park Street of 1787.

Ashley Road – speculative building of 1780–1820 in unrelated pairs and trios.

Berkeley Crescent (1787), a consolation piece in the old style for Thomas Paty on being denied his grand brick crescent.

In this centrepiece for Berkeley Square (1787–92) William Paty demonstrated both his London training and his inexperience.

The threadbare elegance of the Paty's final Neo-classicism – the Georgian House on Great George Street by William Paty of 1790.

Christ Church (1786–90). William Paty's triumphant rehandling of Sir Robert
Taylor's Transfer Offices at the Bank of England of 1765–8.

Home to the most affluent congregation in the city, the Unitarian Chapel at Lewin's Mead (1788–91) by the prison architect, William Blackburn.

Gothick detail on pagoda form, brilliantly innovative yet hopelessly old-fashioned – St Pauls, Hague's centrepiece to Portland Square (1789–94).

A suave exercise in London classicism with Bristol lesenes – Portland Square, north side, by Daniel Hague, begun 1790.

Ashley Place, 1788. Hague's perverse but charming exercise in turning detached houses into a terrace.

FIVE

Merchant Venturer Spring and Economic Frost

The terracing, between 1787 and 1793, of that steep commanding hillside overlooking the Cumberland Basin, was one of the strangest episodes in English building history. Although the cumulative effect of these long rows of houses is nationally celebrated and rightly admired, no one knows for certain the name of a single architect for a single terrace. They were the ruinous architectural triumph of unlucky speculators and bankrupt small-time building firms. Set like a Tibetan lamasery to face the warm south, this first surge of Clifton development was a perfect instance of classical architecture working to a Romantic effect and of orderly units laid down in exhilarating chaos.

Not one of those terraces that look out over the harbour can be ranked among Clifton's five finest. Vyvyan, Worcester, Lansdown Place, Caledonia and the Royal Promenade all lie well back from the hilltop, safely but undramatically settled upon level ground. The early elevations that seized the steep slopes and the most scenic sites are individually mediocre and grossly confused in their positioning; but it is exactly this confusion that generates their excitement and their unique quality. Sunken paths walled down through woodlands, side-slanted roads, roofs apparently underfoot, vertiginous gardens and massive arcades striding above headlong lawns, they all come together to create an urban experience only a stage removed from the original wilderness. Half of Cornwallis's garden is a rough spinney, behind Bellevue is a debris-littered wood, between Prince's Buildings and St. Vincent's Parade a near-precipice of sycamore, ivy and fern crumbles and slides. The people who built and then inhabited these terraces had thoroughly absorbed William Gilpin's theories on the Picturesque. They had no wish to tame Nature, only to enjoy it. This was the Bristol where Robert Southey, Samuel Coleridge and William Wordsworth were exciting the soirées of the merchant gentry in Great George Street. For all its casual classical forms, Clifton is the Romantic Suburb realised.

Bath was order; this first stage of Clifton was serendipity, hence its frustrating anonymity. Royal York Crescent is regularly attributed to William Paty but without a shred of proof and in the teeth of stylistic evidence. William was the cautious innovator who converted polite Bristol to trim rustication, smooth ashlar, delicately pedimented doorcases and correct proportions. Even his father Thomas, if he had been designing on his 1789 deathbed, would never have countenanced such a coarse version of that old, trite recipe of brick lesenes and stepped voussoirs. Royal York's arched doorframes are the cheapest a builder's yard could turn out. The faint projection of the two houses at the mid-point of the forty-six is not a centring, it is a well-concealed visual joke. Yet for all these faults of detail its scale is sensational. It crests the entire hillside and its flagstoned parade could exercise a regiment; no small wonder that the government of 1801 was threatening to turn it into a barracks. The grand solidity of its service area and the fluid curves of those walls above its many access stairways create a substructure much finer than the houses it supports.

For if the engineering is Roman in its scale, the elevations of Royal York, that should, by their building date (1791) have shown at least a hint of neo-Classicism, represent no kind of advance on what the city's journeyman builders had been throwing up ever since the early 1730s. Up there in the endless weather its first brick walls must have leaked like a convict hulk. Render was soon a structural necessity, as were regular coats of paint. Like its fellows on this slope and of this period it is all so amateur. Only Windsor Terrace preserves an absent-minded memory of what the classical orders could convey.

Like so much of Bristol architecture these early Clifton terraces were populist. They express the aspirations of a provincial industrial city with no university and with no aristocratic cultural core. This great building boom of 1787–1793 is often described as a building mania. It was nothing of the sort. The outbreak of the war with France was an artificial shock to a justifiable financial confidence. If Louis XVI had literally kept his head, all the terraces would have been completed briskly and eagerly occupied. They represented a real need, as would be proven by the completion of so many of them before or soon after Waterloo, and by the subsequent successful projection of many more on an equally grander scale and in a more sophisticated style.

In the earlier chapter on the Rococo and Gothick the intense visual and social contrasts of Bristol were mentioned. By 1787 they had become, if anything, more marked. Mediaeval Bristol was never purged by fire as London had been. Caked by centuries of sooty industry it reeked above its tidal mud. It was not only the permanently riotous colliers of Kingswood's seventy pits that the prosperous middle-class was eager to escape. There were collieries even closer, in Bedminster and Easton, and not collieries merely but the black fumes of the glasshouses like that at the foot of Brandon Hill, the ironworks at Ashton Gate and on St. Philip's Marsh and the poisonous smoke from the brass foundries up Crew's Hole. Bristol's working class moreover was notorious for aggression and squalor. Even Mathews's *Guide* with its concentration on sweetness and light, on musical boating parties down the echoing Gorge and raspberry trees in Steeple Ashton, recorded another truth:

> The lowest classes are sharp, witty, droll, saucy, profligate and fraudulent. The common women are numerous, of all dresses, ranks and prices, and nocturnally perambulate as in London. The populace are apt to collect in mobs on the slightest occasions; but have been seldom so spirited as in the late transactions on *Bristol-bridge* (October 1793) where they twice burned the toll-gates and posts, resisted the magistracy and military, prevented the taking of the toll, and at the risque and with the unhappy and lamented loss of several of their lives and limbs (which should, if possible, have been spared,) have perhaps for ever abolished this obnoxious taxation.[1]

Writing this in 1793 Mathews was describing the social environment for the far fiercer Reform Riots of 1831 when something very near to a People's Revolution was staged. The bishop's palace would be wrecked and the mayor's Mansion House burnt, but by then the wise bourgeoisie up at Clifton were safely domiciled. Another witness, James Malcolm, writing this time in 1807, reacted with fascinated despair to the social divide of what is now perhaps the most conservative of English urban areas:

> There are few cities which exhibit a greater contrast in the disposition of their streets, and in the form of their houses, than Bristol. The antient and unaltered parts are inconceivably unpleasant, dark, and dirty; and the suburbs consist of numberless lanes, lined by houses inhabited by a wild race, whose countenances indicate wretchedness and affright. These are the wives and offspring of the labourers at copper and ironworks, glass houses, and many other manufactories; where they are buried from the world, amidst fire, smoke, and dust; and when released, sufficient leisure is denied them to humanize themselves and families.[2]

It was a dark city of dreadful night, but its sharp dualism sprang from the proximity of a high downland paradise fragrant with thyme, prodigal with rare plants and cleansed by salty winds from the sea. Clifton's sudden growth was organic; it was a place of escape where prosperity could distance itself from misery and from the environmental disaster area down by the tidal Avon. This is why Bristol and Clifton were, and to an extent remain, such a binary unit. The activity of 1787–93 was not a building mania, it was an interrupted social imperative.

There were, however, certain events and interested bodies that acted as catalysts to the surge in development. Bristol gossip always flows maliciously about the precise role that the Merchant Venturers, Bristol's shadowy second and unelected City Council, actually play in local affairs. Whether it was by sensitive anticipation or by blundering folly, one way or another this mysterious, though often benevolent, local freemasonry of the wealthy and would-be influential was heavily involved in the sudden growth of Clifton.

By prescient earlier investments the Merchants had become Lords of both the Clifton manors and owners of most of the village land. They were also owners of the Hotwell but had for years leased it out at the very low rent of £5 per annum. As a result the spa had become cheap, lively and raffishly successful. But after suffering a ruinously expensive lawsuit over Champion's Dock,[3] the Merchants, or the 'Hall' as they refer to themselves, tried to recoup their fortunes by raising the rent of the Hotwell and leasing it out to Samuel Powell in 1790.

Powell was the archetypal Clifton investor-developer. While not himself a Merchant, his relatives were powerful in the Hall. A Powell was Master Merchant in 1779, 1795 and 1800. The Merchants throughout the 18th century were very much a family affair, with Eltons, Harfords, Daubenys, Whitchurches and Powells prominent in the recruiting rolls, and families look after their own.

They had spent as much as £3,000 in 1786 on the Hotwell, improving the inconvenient and sewage-surrounded source and building the enchanting little

Doric colonnade of shops with its delicate reeding and detail in striking contrast to the 'horrid' precipice that hangs above it. Samuel Powell was expected, therefore, to make a good return. What he did was virtually to ruin the spa. When Bristolians, who had previously enjoyed free access to their own special tap, were obliged to pay 26 shillings a month for the privilege, they deserted en masse. The water may have been sovereign for old diarrhoeas, hot blood, terminal consumptions, loss of appetite, venereal disease and indigestion, but Bristol was a merchant society and knew the value of money.

This over-pricing was either deplorably or cleverly timed. Clifton, up on its breezy Downs, had always been known and visited for its superior air, but late in the 1780s the hitherto dry village had acquired its own source of hot water. An attorney called Morgan had bought up land on the edge of Sion Hill, which suggests that he was acting with the Merchants' consent. At considerable cost his men had bored down through 250 feet of hard limestone and tapped a spring of water at 70° fahrenheit yielding 34,000 gallons daily. This, the Sion Spring, was made not only to supply a Pump Room and baths, adjacent to the present St. Vincent's Rocks Hotel, but was soon being piped off to three hundred private dwellings. In 1782 William Paty had begun his first terrace, Rodney Place, across the road from his father's earlier Boyce's Buildings. Understandably it was a row of subtle variation in its recessions and its rustication, but so restrained in its effects as to make little visual impact. It was, however, well timed to benefit from the new source. The plundering of the original Hotwell source tends to be underplayed as a significant cause of Clifton's prosperity because both wells, not surprisingly, began to cool, but initially it had a major impact. The 'New Hot Well' is marked on maps from 1793 and by that time Clifton had a set of public rooms to rival the two down at the Hotwell. It was sited in 'Glo'ster Place', the present Gloucester Row, and described as having 'an elegant Ball-room with a good organ and commands a picturesque view of Leigh woods and downs. The whole building is a *capital Hotel*, handsomely fitted up, and extremely well calculated for parties who arrive here, or make excursions for a few days to this delightful spot.'[4]

This, the York House Hotel and Tavern, was demolished long ago, but the New Hot Well Pump Room building survives alongside the main St. Vincent's Rocks Hotel complex, and Sion Hill with Sion Row survive to illustrate the character of the earliest, unplanned speculative development in Clifton during the late 1780s. The lowest seven houses on Sion Hill, down to and including the St. Vincent's Rocks Hotel, have a resounding series of canted bays and bow windows, four and even five storeys high. Standing alongside the New Hot Well within its Pump Room they were designed as lodging houses able to offer superior, highly-priced rooms that commanded wide views of woods and gorge from all their floors. Sion Row has a sequence of large private houses, often with the old style stepped voussoirs. At their backs most of these have canted bays dating back to the years before the houses of West Mall and Caledonia Place blocked their views back over the city. They represent Clifton's last relatively quiet moment before the storm of building came to swell the coffers of the Merchant Venturers. Whether the Hall had deliberately engineered the whole shift of interest upwards to the Downs will never be known, but certainly the Merchants profited by it and at the same time did their city a sterling service.

Samuel Powell had not been Proprietor of the Hotwell for two years before, in December 1792, he was hopelessly in arrears with rent. As he was paying the Hall £900 a year and the highest profit he ever made from his Proprietorship was only £917, his troubles were predictable. But there were other reasons for his financial embarrassment. He must have been better placed than anyone to observe the drift of fashion and when there was news in the local press, late in 1788, that The Mall was shortly to be built on its present site, Powell must have decided to hedge his bets. In May 1789 he leased from the Merchants the land for St. Vincent's Parade on what was then an idyllic site overlooking the Gravel Walk and the Avon, close to the Hotwell, and also the land for Prince of Wales Crescent, now Prince's Buildings, immediately above St. Vincent's Parade but two hundred feet higher and just across the road from the New Hot Well in Clifton. He was already sub-letting in June 1787 and these two, with The Mall, were the first achieved terraces.

They were enough to start off a headlong rush of speculators all eager to invest money in houses with a picturesque outlook and a safe social future. Samuel Powell had only just beaten James Lockier in the race to get a major Clifton project going. Lockier was the most active investor on the strategic hillside. In 1788 he had been gaining experience and expending capital building Berkeley Square, with the builders Davis and Husband, to William Paty's designs. In 1790 he was promoting eighteen houses down in the city in Daniel Hague's Portland Square and again Davis and Husband were active in the same enterprise, building another six houses. It was in this year, 1790, that Lockier got the most grandiose of all the developments, Royal York Crescent, moving. In all these projects, and later in 1791 at St. James's Place on Kingsdown, he never acted alone but always as part of a consortium of investors. In these years there was money around and the mood was optimistic. Work began in 1790 on Saville Place, though only on a fraction, a mere five houses, of a proposed crescent. Finally, in this 'wonderful year', William Watts, the wealthy inventor of the process for producing lead shot from his tower opposite St. Mary Redcliffe, bought a highly unsuitable plot of rocky hillside, not, this time, from the Merchants, but from John Power. He began Windsor Terrace, two houses only as a start to a huge terrace to be poised above the Avon Gorge with a smaller terrace proposed for the hilltop above it.[5] Predictably, 1790 and the year after were both spent pouring the Watts wealth not down a shot-tower, but into the truly cyclopaean foundations which his terrace would require. He never began work on his upper terrace and The Paragon, which would later occupy its site, was not begun until 1809.

Richmond Terrace, in some ways the oddest and least propitious of these ventures, was begun along with York Place and Park Place in the early 1790s, and in 1791 and 1792 the Merchants allowed a hapless attorney, Harry Elderton, to lease from them two more sites. These would eventually become Cornwallis Crescent below Royal York, and Bellevue, that isolated and melancholy row near the Strangers' Grave Yard and Clifton Hill House. Rodney Place had been completed and was occupied with less than the usual trauma because of its close proximity to The Mall and the existing services of Clifton.

The close concern of the Merchant Venturers in all this is illustrated by the haste in which they supported James Lockier when his financial base began to crumble as early as December 1792, before the real panic set in. When a tontine subscription was floated to rescue him no fewer than five of its six trustees, Harford, Fry, Daubeny, Gibbons and Vaughan, were Merchants or became Merchants soon afterwards. As a result, although Royal York Crescent would not be fully occupied for almost thirty years, its long shell was complete before the financial crash of 1793 and stood like a symbol to guarantee the eventual prestige of the whole area.

Such a note of architectural confidence was certainly required. There were more than fifty bankruptcies in the first months of that year after the outbreak of war. Lockier and McAulay went in May, Elderton and his builders at Cornwallis and Bellevue, Messrs. Avard, Lewis and Mitchell, went in August. In all, more than 500 houses were left unfinished. Samuel Powell, with his Merchant connections, survived the storm. In 1792 he had become the salaried Proprietor, not the leaseholder, of the failing Hotwell and in 1796 he mortgaged his Prince's Buildings to William Paty, thereby avoiding bankruptcy. When the century came in he and his son John, an auctioneer of Dowry Square, were picking up the shells of houses cheaply and completing them.[6] By 1812 they had lodging houses in Windsor Terrace, numbers 3-7 in Hope Square, The Mall, Granby Place, Sion Row, Glo'ster Row, Beaufort Cottages and three still in Prince's Buildings. It was an ill financial wind that blew no good to a friend of the Merchants. The Powells represent the continuity behind the apparent collapse and the basic soundness of the whole Clifton enterprise.

On stylistic evidence St. Vincent's Parade and The Mall were both to William Paty's design. They share certain features, a split keystone in their rustication together with the rather old-fashioned sill-course that he used in Berkeley Square. Rodney Place was also by William Paty. John Eveleigh, the Bath architect of Camden Crescent, may well have provided William Watts with the original rich design for Windsor Terrace. Later incompetents were to apply the most improbable variations to this but they created, perversely, the most interesting terrace in Bristol, one that seizes even the most casual attention by the failure of its expensively carved pilasters to make their obvious connections to the entablature. Eveleigh's other two projects were the first five houses of Saville Place and Beaufort Buildings which was much later. All three terraces employ round arches set deeply within their rustication and have, consequently, an air of worldly stability unusual in this part of Clifton.

The terraces built to the cheapest designs, York Place and Richmond Terrace (or Place as it is sometimes called) seem to have been in occupation early,[7] as if costs had been cut to the bone in order to have premises for sale – Richmond Terrace's builders must have consumed much of their initial capital on the three immense ranges of substructure. The mystery is why they should have bothered when the additional height so gained produced no dividend in views and the site was perfectly level to begin with. Nothing was spent to improve the three-sided and distinctly tenement-like ranges that face into its rear square.

Bellevue, Cornwallis and, later, The Paragon, were all designed in such a way that their expensive elevations became part of the picturesque landscape while their entrance façades were relatively humble. Cornwallis was a notable dualistic creation. Its convex entrance elevation looking into the hill-slope is even more impoverished than that of Royal York. It is of rendered brick with stepped voussoirs and lacks even the relief of lesenes. This must be the design that Harry Elderton persuaded his builders to use in a vain attempt to avoid the bankruptcy that overtook them all in 1793. When the Greenways leased some of the wreck in 1809 they too were already on the edge of bankruptcy. Olive and John Greenway, of that firm, survived the proceedings and continued to build, so the far superior concave face of Cornwallis looking out onto its precipitous garden may be their design. It is ashlar-faced with banded rustication and creates, with its grand terrace, a remarkable private world that can only be viewed from a mile or more away and then through a veil of trees.

James Malcolm saw these terraces and houses set among 'picturesque inequalities', 'rich groups of trees' and 'verdant slopes of grass' as the kind of scene that Morland 'would have correctly and finely delineated'.[8] There does seem in at least these three cases to have been a conscious effort to make the terraces respond pictorially to their landscape. The Paragon's garden, or more correctly precipice, elevation has an extrovert elegance of ashlar, rustication and balconies that is spent entirely on the desert air. Its street front, before the Greek Revival porches were added, was a very dim and inward affair, lumpish with heavy architraves. John Drew, the builder who perpetrated the wings to Windsor Terrace, is recorded as having raised The Paragon's first ten houses before he too went bankrupt in 1813. But the complete stylistic contrast between its precipice and its street elevations makes it probable that Stephen Hunter, the builder who completed the terrace, refaced the whole street side. The splendid return house at the end is literally viewable only by hang-glider pilots: an airy classical castle that revels in its position.

The tragic hero of these middle years of Clifton development was Francis Greenway. He was transported to Australia for forgery before he was able to complete the Hotel and Assembly Rooms in The Mall, and so set the seal on Clifton's superior social order. It is curious how the ghost of William Halfpenny, so frustrated and ineffective in his lifetime, continued to haunt Bristol long after his death. St. Paul's church reads like his posthumous achievement, and Greenway's loutishly personable Assembly Rooms owe the whole relationship of their squat rusticated basement and their attic propped on a giant order of Ionic columns to

Halfpenny's far better proportioned, though equally odd, Coopers' Hall in King Street. Greenway's long elevation with this defiant five-bay centrepiece, two three-storey bows and six other inconsequential retreats and advances can be most charitably interpreted as an attempt to make clear the several functions of hotel, public rooms and housing. Within there is a ballroom, a raw Greek Revival space with painted red marble columns, Tower of the Winds capitals and that unmistakable Regency air of skin-deep affluence. It was the work of Joseph Kay who took over when Greenway's troubles begain in 1809.

In 1813 Francis Greenway's death sentence was commuted to transportation for life and he left to begin a new role as the Father of Australian Architecture. His involuntary departure marks a sobering end to a gimcrack period of improvisation and haste in Bristol building. But at least he left a solid, if idiosyncratic, show of columns behind him as a foretaste of the highly individual neo-Classicism which was about to take the sluggard city in a late, prodigious flowering.

CHAPTER FIVE – NOTES

1 W. Mathews, *New History, Survey and Description of the City and Suburbs of Bristol and Guide to the Hotwells and Clifton* (Bristol, 1793), pp. 90–1.
2 Malcolm, p.195.
3 For the lawsuit see Patrick McGrath, *The Merchant Venturers of Bristol* (Bristol, 1975), pp.154–7.
4 Mathews, p.104.
5 A view of the Gorge showing the proposed upper terrace above Windsor and the original crescent form of Windsor itself was published in the Bristol *Evening Post*, 3 June 1986.
6 The unfinished houses and the completed Royal York Crescent are shown in a view of St. Vincent's Rocks in Malcolm, opposite p.249.
7 In 1805, eight houses in York Place were complete and by 1809 the whole terrace was in occupation.
8 Malcolm, p.194.

Clifton – the lamasery effect of repetitive units dramatised by a site that almost raises modern flats to fine architecture.

Wilderness and sophistication, the essence of Clifton's attraction for devotees of the picturesque –
balconied rear elevations to Prince's Buildings.

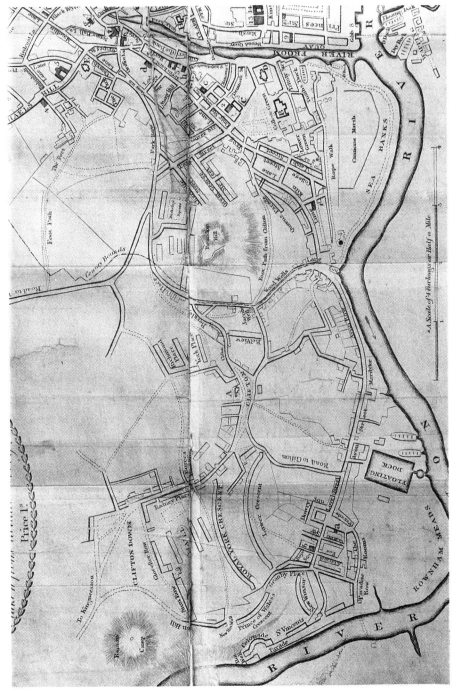

Clifton in 1794 from Matthews' Guide. Much that is shown remained incomplete throughout the war years.

Superb in scale, trivial in detail –
Royal York Crescent (1791–1820)
rescued by its grand substructure
and ironwork.

The Colonnade was built in 1786
in a last attempt to inject a note
of fashionable parade and
commerce into the cramped and
declining Hotwell.

128

Sion Hill in its 1780–90 unregulated years with bow-fronted lodging houses at the lower end by the New Hot Well.

Where The Mall of 1789 by William Paty links with West Mall and its Grecian ironwork by Foster and Okely, begun about 1832.

Prince's Buildings, begun in 1789 for the proprietor of the Hotwell when his spa was losing to the superior charms of the heights above.

A Bath design gloriously mismanaged by Bristol builders – Windsor Terrace, begun in 1790.

The ashlared inner face of Cornwallis Crescent (begun 1791) strides grandly along its massive terraced base, above its own private wood.

Richmond Terrace (1790) wrecked by later refacings and window alterations.

The stone-faced convex of The Paragon – conventional late 18th century styling of 1809–13 on a wholly unconventional site.

Heavy architraves and dull render on the Paragon's concave rescued by later porches.

William Halfpenny's tradition of perverse proportions continued by Francis Greenway in the
Clifton Assembly Rooms, begun in 1806.

The Assembly Ballroom – completed by Joseph Kay with true Regency panache in 1809 after Greenway's transportation as a convict.

SIX

An Incursion of Architects – Bristol before the Riots

Those periods of classical building that can honestly be described as 'a renaissance' by their quality are not easy phenomena to explain. They seem to arise from a sudden delighted appreciation of the potential in Greek or Roman forms and decorative detail, but there has also to be some cheerful indifference as to the precise rules by which these must be organised. The Saintonge in the Aquitaine had such a renaissance in the 12th century, Mantua in the 15th, the Loire valley in the 16th and there are a number of other spontaneous and usually celebrated responses to the old themes. England has never enjoyed a renaissance of building on a national scale. The island has been too remote from the classical sources and consequently over-anxious to be correct, too eager to follow the rules of Palladio, Serlio or Scamozzi, the authority rather than the spirit. John Wood's Bath and Robert Adam's Edinburgh New Town are great classical achievements but neither could be described as a creative Springtime. But in the narrow compass of its north-west suburban heights and from 1810 until perhaps 1853, Bristol did indulge in a glorious classical free-for-all to which the title of at least a renaissance in miniature can plausibly be applied.

The city had a long tradition of mercantile philistinism, coarsened by an aggressive Protestant instinct for self-denial. Its renaissance came late, after a century of provincial conservatism, and it appears to have had no patrons or prime movers. Significantly, the whole exhilarating episode has been subsequently down-slanted, as if a serious trading and industrial city were almost embarrassed by an achievement so out of character. Not one of the architects behind it all – the Fosters, Okely, Dyer, Pope, Underwood – is remembered with honour in the city. Indeed there has been almost a conspiracy of oblivion. It is inconceivable that the designer of a terrace like Lansdown Place would have been forgotten if it had been built in London, Bath or Newcastle. But in Bristol the origins and exact dates not only of Lansdown but of a whole wealth of villas, pairs and terraces in the streets around are for the most part obscure. By the habit of carving his name and a date on those buildings of which he was most proud, Charles Dyer seems to have assessed the memory span of the citizens very shrewdly.

Nothing of the first 1787–1793 building drive, except the amazing Piranesian wreck of Windsor Terrace, was consciously aimed at a classical image. Those other rows and terraces were orderly and by their siting on a wooded hillside they were accidentally picturesque, but nothing more. When they were built the casual eclectic scholarship, usually described as 'Regency', had not reached Bristol. Then, after 1800, there was the long consolidation of what had been thrown up so quickly. In a buyer's market there was little chance for stylistic innovation. Work went on sometimes, as at The Paragon and Cornwallis Crescent, of completion, but usually, as at Royal York, St. James's Parade and York Place, merely of fitting out. Everywhere there were completed shells of houses waiting for the plasterers. Richmond Terrace, for instance, was set with man-traps which ran with blood in 1799 when a gang of lead thieves ventured in unwisely. As late as 1828 only five houses in Park Place were inhabited, though the shells had been in place by 1793. Unlucky Cornwallis, long known simply as the Lower Crescent, was still being fitted up in 1835.

Harley Place illustrates the tentative experimentalism of that first decade of the new century. Its terraced substructure had been in place at the time of the panic in 1793 and the lower four houses, built to an original design, sit soberly on this. But as the terrace mounts, some of the houses play with shallow geometrical panels until the top-most house, number 9, ventures to be truly Soaneian in its eccentric lightness, yet still manages to be contained within the rhythm of the pilaster lesenes of the row.

Bristol always needed outsiders, real architects, to rescue it from the builder-contractors. It was the Commercial Rooms in Corn Street, built in 1810–11 and designed by the Londoner, Charles Busby (1788–1834), that began to nudge the prosperous, potential house builders of the city into an awareness of both the Greek Revival and perhaps illogically, of the possibilities of structural frivolity.

Businessmen of the city had become aware that it was no longer normal practice to seal bargains by striking a brass baluster in the middle of the street. So, with a curious faith in inexperience, they went to the twenty-one year old Busby to design them a club-room in which their London or Liverpool partners would feel at home. Busby had published in 1808 a book of villa designs 'adapted with Economy to the Comforts and to the Elegancies of Modern Life',[1] but his only real achievement to that date had been Nightingale Cottage off Clapham Common. The faith of the original five hundred subscribers to the Rooms paid off, and for £17,000 Busby gave them a 'great room' of flashy elegance which has worked splendidly ever since. Over this luncheon room is a glazed lantern supported by twelve maidens (caryatids inspired by those on the Erechtheion at Athens) with their hands demurely crossed over their breasts. Rich and light as a well-cooked pudding, this airy structure rests on a ceiling coffered with delicate Vitruvian scroll patterning. Light streaming down from above, hints of gold and mahogany and an Ionic buffet near the kitchens all create a sense of gentlemanly opulence. On the wall a wind dial brings to mind merchant argosies sailing up the Bristol Channel. Within months of its completion a hundred new members had joined. The innovation was an immediate success.

The chaste Ionic portico through which these six hundred possible house builders entered their club would have given them a taste for Greek temple features as a normal background to everyday life. Over the doors a frieze represents Neptune offering tribute to Britannia and if J. G. Bubb, who carved it, had to rely for the shape of his camel on the beasts that Thomas Paty had carved so long before on the Exchange, then the drapery of his figures at least was correctly Grecian.

That temple detail would find echoes on porches and windows all over Clifton in the next forty years, but the example was not immediately absorbed into domestic practice and it would be another eleven years before two far more prestigious outside architects, Sir Robert Smirke and Charles Cockerell, were invited to design within the guarded circle of the city limits.

The citizenry must have felt that they had had a lucky escape when Charles Busby fled to America in 1814 to avoid bankruptcy proceedings after the collapse of some of his iron-constructed ceilings. His floating dome over the Commercial Rooms remained secure and Busby himself, after studying the oddly-related topics of American state penitentiaries and propulsion units for paddle-steamers, returned to create a successful practice in Brighton. Sadly, he never designed again in Bristol.

After William Paty's death in 1800 the natural successor to his extensive practice was James Foster the Elder (1748–1823), first of a long and prosperous line of architect Fosters in Bristol. He had been William Paty's apprentice and became the favoured surveyor and architect of the Merchant Venturers. Stylistically he was conservative, as would be expected in a Paty pupil, but he was aware of Sir John Soane's innovations. The strange half-terrace, half-semi-detached line of houses that stumbles up Richmond Hill was designed by James Foster after 1821. The basements of the semi-terrace are rusticated in the William Paty manner but the upper floors aim at Soaneian geometry with windows set in shallow recessed arches and bald, bare parapets. A signature of James Foster's designs is a channelled or anthemion-incised pilaster that never seems to end in a capital or to summon up enough strength to reach the pediment which it should support. But in their lean, spare way the first houses up Richmond Hill are handsome enough though the Bristol bourgeois would soon be demanding more ornate elevations for his money.

In 1822 Benjamin Tucker leased the Honeypen Hill property from the Merchants and they made it a condition that the seventeen houses of Meridian Place and fifteen cottages should be built to James Foster's designs.[2] The paired villas of Richmond Hill Avenue are survivors of these cottages. Stucco-finished and linked together under wispy pediments, they cling to a faint ghost of classical design, their shallow blind windows and the inevitable channelled pilasters lending a slight Soaneian elegance. Tucker's seventeen 'tenement' houses must have been a financial success for he shortly built another fourteen on Frederick Place, narrow, cut-price houses like those on Meridian Place, dignified by an excessively thin pediment at one end.

The elder James Foster died in 1823 and it would have been his sons, Thomas and a second James who seized upon Smirke's Council House design in 1824 to build the Arcades in a new, confident Greek classicism. But years later the old style mason-builder William Pennington was still designing and building in the style of the elder James Foster. Oakfield Place, the related section of St. Paul's Road and Southleigh Road were all built by Pennington, still with a few anthemion incisions.[3]

Another last terraced effort in the old, tame minimalism, cutting every economic corner but retaining a certain impoverished elegance, was The Polygon, just above Dowry Square. This was begun in 1826, the same year as Freeland Place below Windsor Terrace. The former turns its best face perversely into a green bank, its slovenly rear to the vistas, while Freeland flows easily down, with no attempt to keep up appearances. Only Wellington Place, of all these late hillside terraces, breaks away from conventional fenestration and risks one or two of the tripartite windows that were soon to be standard in the Clifton of the 1830s and 1840s. That little curve of houses under the great lee-wave of Royal York was begun in 1821, but its pioneering windows cannot be precisely dated.

If Clifton during the early 1820s was a place of stylistic reserve and indecision, in the city at least there was movement. Sir Robert Smirke's new chapel of ease for St. Augustine's and Charles Cockerell's Philosophical and Literary Institute on Park Street, both begun in 1821, were markers to innovation and neither was a building that could easily be ignored. Athens and Greek independence were in the national air at that date and, rather as Bristol had to have its Commercial Rooms in 1810 to keep up with Liverpool's Lyceum, so in 1821 any British city with pretensions to status had somehow to associate itself with the Acropolis.

Perhaps St. George's, Brandon Hill, as the chapel of ease soon became, has never been a greatly loved building, but as stage scenery and a symbol it is formidable. Recently secularised and used as a concert hall, it would more fittingly house an elected chief executive of unlimited authority and almost god-like civil powers. Discreetly ruined it would be unforgettable. No matter that it was only raised on that slope because there was a spare graveyard and no real congregation to justify a church, or that its structure became acutely dysfunctional as soon as its congregation went High Church. No matter that its tremendous flight of steps and lowering Doric portico were only a back entrance to the vestries. Together with Cockerell's semi-circular peristyle a little lower down the hill, it associated Greek columns with Civic Consequence in the public mind. Hence came the sequence of great houses out on the Downs, the funeral lodges of Arno's Vale Cemetery and the brilliant portico of the Victoria Rooms that still holds the upper Queen's Road with such grace and authority.

More immediately these two portentous portals inspired the Royal Colonnade, a group of four, three-bay, houses that try engagingly at the foot of St. George's steps to look like a Bristol version of Carlton House. By the boldness of its conception, its flagrant disregard for classical rules and the weakness of its fenestration, this has to be the first Bristol design (it was up in 1828) by Richard Shackleton Pope.

Along with the Fosters, Charles Dyer and Charles Underwood, Pope created the Clifton Renaissance and like Dyer he was the son of an influential Bristolian. Of the four architectural firms, only Underwood came from outside. Pope's father, Thomas had served as Smirke's clerk of works at the Royal Mint and been a district surveyor in Bristol. Pope himself had also worked under Smirke and returned to Bristol to superintend Cockerell's Philosophical Institute. Even without these pointers to his authorship the Royal Colonnade previews some of Pope's favourite elevational tricks. The dramatic projection of its three-bay wings and the deep shadows of its Ionic colonnade were a trial run for his Royal Western Hotel (1837–9), now Brunel House, as were its notably fussy and un-Greek window architraves. As for the lively rhythm of that colonnade which has offended purists from Pevsner onwards, its pattern is a marker for Pope as the designer of Dorset and Alva House, that wonderfully upsetting pair out on the Clifton Downs. These were built in 1829–30, soon after the Royal Colonnade, and their rhythm of columns is as confidently incorrect. Seen as a chain reaction, of outsiders affecting Bristol-born architects with London experience, the sequence of St. George's and the Institute (1821), Royal Colonnade (*c*.1826) and Dorset-Alva (1829–30) illustrates exactly how Clifton building styles of the 1830s and 1840s got their inspiration and their wilful originality.

Meanwhile the ever-corrupt City Corporation were edging into the architectural scene for the first time since their disastrous dictats over Queen Square in 1699. In 1823, not to be outdone by the Anglican Church, they commissioned Smirke to design them a new Council House on the Corn Street–Broad Street corner and proceeded, more surprisingly, to actually build it from 1824 to 1827. The dates are important because already in 1824 the most active and influential of the city's architectural dynasties, the Fosters, had stolen Smirke's design quite shamelessly and used his Ionic columns *in antis* with a dense Greek frieze of stylized anthemion and giant pilasters as the major entranceways into their Upper and Lower Arcades. Only the Lower Arcade has survived the bombing of 1940, but the quality of its portals and the elegance of the arcaded shops within are enough to show how the two Arcades must have transformed the whole style of Bristol shopping when they were completed in 1826, a whole year ahead of the Council House. Here again an outside architect has brought an introverted architectural practice to life.

Not that there was anything sensational in the national sense about Smirke's Council House. Not only was it a repeat of his Royal College of Physicians (1824–7) in Trafalgar Square,[4] but it became an immediate laughing stock in Bristol for the lopsided line of its front to Corn Street and the brown Pompeian gloom of its top-lit Council Chamber.[5]

A certain frisson of scandalized pleasure is inevitable at any mention of the affairs of Bristol Corporation. At this time its members were still entirely unreformed and, if anything, more corrupt and self-indulgent than when they were last noticed in the first decade of the 18th century. The difference was that, with the general body of the citizens better educated and more critical, they were now extremely unpopular. The most striking fact about the Bristol Riots of 1831 that devastated the Queen Square area was that a gang of a mere fifty to a hundred youths and Irish labourers, looted and burnt the mayor's Mansion House and the merchant houses around it while a crowd of at least a thousand respectable citizens simply watched the lawless spectacle as if they were at the Theatre Royal enjoying an expensively staged epic drama.

Quite simply everything that the Corporation touched had turned to either ashes or alcohol. The constant presence in the city of the powerful but shadowy Merchant Venturers seems to have absolved the City Council from its real responsibilities. They had delayed any improvements to the harbour while Liverpool overtook Bristol as a trading port. Then when the Floating Harbour was created after the expensive works on the New Cut and opened in 1809, the harbour dues that were imposed in an effort to produce a dividend for the investors were so steep that captains avoided the port whenever possible. A cargo of Spanish quicksilver that could dock in Liverpool for £10.8s.4d. would have been charged £33.6s.1d. in Bristol.

Despite the decline in trade and consequently in income, the councillors voted an alderman's widow £100 a year for life in 1817, another £60 in 1820. The mayor's allowance was raised to £2,500 in 1813 and in 1816 Sir William Struth was awarded £3,346 for condescending to serve a second term. While the city's Grammar School had shrunk to one pupil the Corporation could spend £700 on a ball and a banquet at which thirty-five separate toasts were drunk and the glee 'With a Jolly Full Bottle' roared out in chorus.

Most of the Corporation were also habitués of the Commercial Rooms and it was probably the top-lighting of the one that made the councillors eager to have a Council House in something of the same style. That they spent only £16,000 on their House compared with the £17,000 spent seventeen years before on the Commercial Rooms might seem a sign of good husbandry were it not for the fact that they had to borrow £10,000 in 1827-8, then spent £802 on pipes of port and Madeira. Between 1824 and 1835 £18,000 was improperly withdrawn from charities by which time Corporation debts had mounted to £90,000. With strangely prophetic insight into the nights of fire that were to rage in 1831, they had spent £5,200 in 1829 on a proposed new Mansion House in Great George Street with a fine view up to Smirke's ponderous Greek portico. Yet no one appears to have noticed that the earth was trembling.

Unless, that is, the building of the first ten houses out along the Downs at Clifton on Litfield Place and the Promenade, all constructed before the Riots of 1831, was carried through by men wealthy and wise enough to distance themselves from the coming storm. It is certainly a coincidence that the grandest of these, Camp House, signed and dated on its balcony, 1831, by Charles Dyer, was the home of Charles Pinney who was actually the mayor at the time of the Riots, lost all his glass, crockery and linen in the wreck of the Mansion House and only escaped with his life by crawling along a gutter and breaking into the Customs House by an attic window.

Although Glasgow has fine houses of this period and there are many of the same scale and style near Regent's Park in London, no British city has a continuous sequence to match the chain from Litfield House to the present Mansion House. Each building is distinctive and often daringly inventive like a row of trendy country houses all set in one park and overlooking a romantic intensity of woods and rocky gorge. Invented by a novelist it would be dismissed as improbably un-English.

142

It began relatively mildly with the six houses in three pairs next to Litfield House, which is number one, though the last to be built of the seven. These first six were all built before 1828, marked on Ashmead's map of that date when Litfield's own plot is still shown as empty. Since Litfield House itself was designed by Charles Dyer in 1830 (it has his usual carved signature and date) there is a possibility that he had a hand in the adjoining six. The first pair (numbers 2 and 3) are, however, a throwback to the 1790 austerities of Great George Street. Their reserve is icy, a thin cornice and a sill-band can hardly be described as notes of relief, but here the tripartite windows, finely detailed, on the ground floor are being used confidently to give the facade's ground-base some distinction. The ironwork of the long pergola with its anthemions over the supports does much to pull the two-storey wings and three-storey centre together. The elevation remains, nevertheless, wintry. Numbers 4 and 5 are large but, by the standards of what was to come, commonplace, their porches of Ionic columns set *in antis* to show that Smirke's device at the Council House had been noted. On the last pair (numbers 6 and 7) the banded rustication and the setting of plain pilasters in twos to articulate the facade marks a trial run of features that were to be lavished indiscriminately on Clifton houses for the next thirty years or more. The porches of this pair are actually emphasised by four pilasters apiece. Here again Smirke had led the way by using pairs of pilasters, though with much richer capitals, on the Broad Street elevation of the Council House.

Next door to number 7 are Dorset and Alva, the pair already noted and attributed on their style alone to Pope, reworking even more daringly the theme of an attic supported on a giant order which Francis Greenway had used at the Clifton Assembly Rooms. So with Pope and the Fosters already active and experimental, Charles Dyer, the third of the four key architects in Bristol's late classical flowering, arrives tardy but hyperactive with Litfield House. When he died aged fifty-four in 1848 his death would be ascribed to 'paralysis induced by too close application.'[6]

Litfield House, Oakfield House and Camp House, packed together between 1829 and 1831, are a real proof of Bristol's architectural awakening. Though they were all by Dyer, they have very few similarities. Here at last, after the long decades when one feeble feature is made to serve its turn on any number of houses or terraces, is an architect prodigal of invention and lavish with detail. Dyer has mastered Hellenic ornament but wholly disregarded Hellenic disciplines. Litfield House has four fully modelled facades, only one in stone, the others stucco. Its elevation to the road brims with tensions and contradictions and makes an ideal introduction to the stylistic riot of the years ahead. The porch has impeccable Greek detail but sets its perfect Doric columns incorrectly in pairs and mocks the whole feature by a balustrade and balconies of Doric columns in miniature. This particular joke must have amused Dyer and his clients as he sets the Lilliputian colonnades into the parapets of Oakfield House and Camp House. Further evidence of Dyer's defiant indiscipline comes from the fenestration. All three floors of Litfield employ a different pattern with the tripartite beginning now to become standard for the best rooms on the ground floor. All four pairs of pilasters on the top two floors are needed to give coherence to the facade and distract the attention from the civil war of windows. Their capitals are of that essentially 'Regency' type, common in Cheltenham and some London suburbs. Often described as Greek or Corinthian, they are in fact wildly composite and can be varied with any kind of flower or paterae that the architect wishes to set among volutes and overgrown acanthus.

In Camp House, Mayor Pinney's Gorge-side hideaway, the mood is bewilderingly different. Litfield was a box, its elevations relatively two-dimensional. Camp House lunges out towards the road with a deep, double-decker portico, correct again in detail but outrageous as an ensemble. Doric below, Ionic above, the 2/1/1/2 rhythm of the columns creates some suspicion that perhaps Dyer rather than Pope may have designed the Dorset-Alva pair up the hill. When every architect is unpredictable the architectural historian is necessarily often at a loss. That is the delight of late Clifton, but one reason for its being so regularly under-played in architectural textbooks. It frightens the experts, and with good reason.

On Camp House Dyer lets his fenestration run wild again. The sharply-cut windows of the central three bays bear no relation to the two floors of tripartites on the wings and there is neither rime nor reason to the juxtapositioning of heavy pediments on the first floor of the wings to the meagre rectangles sliced into the frieze that light the second floor. A final kick in the teeth of expectations is delivered by a pedimented Doric porch set casually to the side.

Oakfield is the mystery house of these three. Far away from the grand downland houses, it appears for the first time on Ashmead's map of 1833, beside a country lane from Clifton to Cotham. Never documented as a Dyer house, its coupled pilasters and the Doric miniatures of its parapet proclaim rather than suggest his hand. But of the three houses this was probably the first and it may have been his introduction to Bristol building in about 1829. His father, George Dyer, was not only a wealthy local surgeon but, by the fact that he had laid the ceremonial foundation stone of the Commercial Rooms back in 1810, an enthusiast for architectural experiment. Charles could well have owed early commissions like Oakfield to his father's friends. Compared with Litfield and Camp, Oakfield has relatively normal fenestration, its windows being handled exactly like those on the first floor of Litfield. Where Camp House charges forward with a double portico, Oakfield attacks its visitors with a boldly projecting tower and a porch with Tower of the Winds capitals, at the same time it encloses them within a forecourt.

All in all those diverse houses make a promising prelude to the great Riots of 1831, the drunken bonfire banquets of the mob and the panic-stricken flight of the affluent. When mansions like these with ample grounds could be raised on the edge of fine landscapes, the plain brick boxes of Queen Square, jostled by slums and reeking from the sewage-ridden harbour, had few charms. It is an ill riot that can blow no commissions in the way of an enterprising architect.

The Fosters, Pope and Dyer had all now cut their teeth on commissions and Charles Underwood, the wiser for an 1821 bankruptcy in Cheltenham, had set up office hopefully in Exchange Buildings in 1828. Outsiders were to have one more major opportunity when Charles Cockerell who had, to be fair, faced an impossible task with his Philosophical Institute on the steeps of Park Street, was asked in 1829 to design a new church, Holy Trinity, for the Hotwells.

He raised it at precisely the time when the social status of the little spa had collapsed. Its interior was what St. Stephen Walbrook might have looked like if it had been designed by Soane instead of Wren, but wartime bombs have destroyed it. Because the exterior is bold, almost Vanbrughian, in its central narthex and quite un-church-like in feeling, it tends to be praised for its spatial qualities. It has, however, left no heirs in a city where the moneyed classes were becoming intoxicated, not by serious voids and solemn planes of 'thoughtful' masonry, but by the undisciplined richness of a classical vocabulary long held back from them, and now at last made available to them by a new generation of seductive designers.

So the political thunderheads of the great Reform Bill gathered about a city, no longer perhaps the second in the land, but still an urban unit of over 100,000 souls strongly radical as an inheritance of its noncomformist past. Bristol's Recorder and chief legal authority, Sir Charles Wetherell, had become a hero of the city in 1829 for speaking out against Roman Catholics. In August 1831 his popularity plummeted when he declared in Parliament that 'the Reform fever had a good deal abated in Bristol'.[7] Radical elements of the population determined to disabuse him on that matter.

On Saturday 29 October Sir Charles was due to make his state entrance into the city with the Sheriffs to open the Assize. Trouble was expected, but when an attempt was made to swear in 300 extra constables, respectable gentlemen and tradesmen for the most part refused. As Sir Charles's coach rolled in from Totterdown the Corporation's minds may have been set upon the usual welcoming banquet and carousel: the turtle soup, the sides of beef, the oysters and the geese already preparing in the Mansion House kitchens. Afterwards there would be merry drinking catches to accompany the port. But in Temple Street an angry crowd of almost two thousand was waiting. That night the beef, the oysters and the port would be consumed by uninvited guests from the meanest slums of the city, low alleys in the Pithay, the Dings and Baptist Mills. When the fury of the next three days had subsided neither social Bristol nor its familiar architectural setting would ever be quite the same again.

CHAPTER SIX - NOTES

1 Quoted in Colvin, p.175; Busby's book is entitled: *A Series of Designs for Villas and Country Houses.*

2 The Merchant Venturers' Hall Book 15 for 4 July 1822 (pp.238–9) states that the 'specification of the whole of the work [is to be] prepared by Messrs. Foster'.

3 Three houses at the north-east corner of Buckingham Vale also have incised anthemions and may well be by Pennington.

4 Smirke's building, much altered, is now Canada House.

5 A contemporary verse asked:
　'Why yonder Mansion stands awry,
　Does Bristol wondering seek –
　Like to its Council is its Site,
　Oblique – Oblique – Oblique!'

6 Quoted from Dyer's obituary notice in the *Builder* (1848), p. 54.

7 John Latimer, *The Annals of Bristol in the Nineteenth Century* (1887), p. 146.

9 Harley Place, with Soaneian lightness of touch at the top of a gently experimental terrace.

A semi-detached villa pair on Richmond Hill of about 1822 in the elder James Foster's gaunt, frail Regency classicism.

Charles Busby's Commercial Rooms (1810–11) were a diminutive but strategically sited introduction of the Greek Revival to Bristol.

Rich and light as a well-cooked pudding – Busby's caryatid-supported dome in the Commercial Rooms.

Not more awful around Paradise the walls of sacred Death. At St George, Brandon Hill
(1823) Robert Smirke taught Bristol to speak Greek.

A brilliant distraction from the uneasy siting of a building – Charles Cockerell's 1821 portico on Park Street.

The Royal Colonnade (1828) a self-willed, self-confident exercise in erratic classical rhythms by Richard Shackleton Pope.

Before Sir Robert Smirke's Council House (1824–7) had been completed elements of its design appeared in the Fosters' 1824 Arcades.

Dorset and Alva House of 1829–30 in the bold Bristol tradition of treating the classical orders with creative contempt.

Litfield House, 1830. An apparently orderly Greek box alive with the tensions and contradictions that were a Charles Dyer characteristic.

Charles Dyer's Camp House of 1831 – correct in detail but outrageous as an ensemble and, below, Oakfield House carries the Dyer signature of aggressive spatial thrust and inconsequential fenestration.

Holy Trinity, Hotwells (1829). Cockerell's church offered confident simplicities just as Clifton acquired a taste for rich complexities.

SEVEN

The Clifton Renaissance after the Great Riots

Images of the riots of 1831 soon became part of Bristol's enduring folk memory. Most of the houses that were burnt on the north and west sides of Queen Square were incendiarised by eleven year old urchins scrambling from window to window along the coping. A single maidservant, Martha Davis, saved the Cross house simply by directing the rioters to the door by the scruffs of their necks. One hour of decisive action by Colonel Brereton and his Dragoons on that first Saturday would have sobered the city. Instead a scene worthy of John Martin's wildest canvases was allowed to develop. 'One seemed', Charles Kingsley wrote later, 'to look down upon Dante's Inferno, and to hear the multitudinous moan and wail of the lost spirits surging to and fro amid that sea of fire',[1] and his words recapture the horrified relish with which respectable Bristol seems to have absorbed the event.

It was, when its basic triviality and avoidability is accepted, still Britain's closest approximation to the French Revolution. A bishop's palace, a mansion house, a customs house, two gaols and half the largest residential square in England, all destroyed, was a fairish score for one weekend of activity by a mob of drunken, unarmed colliers, Irish labourers and small boys. The social and therefore the architectural message was clear. Prosperous Bristolians would be safer and happier isolated from the lower orders and surrounded by their own kind. They took, literally, to the hills. Clifton after 1831 was basically a Tory redoubt fortified by wide roads and grand elevations, cut off from the rest of the city by Park Street's impregnable glacis. The Victoria Rooms were originally founded as the Conservative Rooms. Vyvyan Terrace was named defiantly after the Tory MP Sir Richard Vyvyan who won the 1832 parliamentary election by defying the Reform Bill, bribing twelve hundred voters with £1.3s. apiece and promising them 7 lbs of 'blue beef' each next Christmas.

Queen Square was rebuilt quickly. It is impossible to pretend that its partial destruction was any great architectural loss. Sir Robert Smirke was too busy and recommended his son, Sydney, to design a new Customs House. This had no open loggia but long, melancholy round-headed windows that appear to light a two-storey upper hall but are structurally contradicted by the windows of the side elevation. Henry Rumley rebuilt the burnt houses with a frigid elegance of fine ashlar enlivened by pilaster capitals of the type sometimes called 'Grecian' but which would be more accurately described as Regency floral baskets.

All the real activity and the imaginative design had moved now up into Clifton. Charles Dyer was the prime mover and Richard Pope was close behind him; even the Fosters had sensed the way the building market was moving. Together they made 1832 the annus mirabile for the rising suburb and began the golden decades of Clifton. This was the year when Dyer proposed and designed what would become the Victoria Rooms as the social and eminently visual nexus for a new Bristol. Confident his plans would be accepted and that the site would become prime for development he rushed up three pairs of villas, Kingston, Freshford, Widcombe, Bedford, Thornton and Edgecumbe on the strip of land between Richmond Hill and the new extension to Queen's Road.

'Sumptuous' is the mildest adjective to describe them. In compressed grandeur and in their carefree handling of classical motifs they set a new standard for surburban aspirations. In 1833, the year of their completion, John Decimus Pountney, joint partner with the Goldneys in a firm of earthenware manufacturers, and soon, in 1847, to be mayor of Bristol, bought Freshford. Mrs. Elton, a widow from that dynasty of patrician aldermen, took Thornton. In villas and terraces all around them lived admirals, sons of local MPs, bar-iron and tinplate merchants, attorneys and wool factors. Farway House, third from the lower end of Richmond Hill, was the house of Lord John Somerset with the final cachet for Bristol of Badminton and the Dukes of Beaufort. The area had arrived.

For Pope and the Foster partnership success was not quite so immediate but it was in 1832 that Pope began to build Vyvyan, greatest, grandest and least digestible of all Clifton terraces. Dim but persistent, Thomas Foster and his partner William Okely began in the same hopeful year to build West Mall from its eastern end, Caledonia Place from the west and Clifton Vale from the top of its hill downwards, all to accommodate the migrant middle-classes as they abandoned the old city. Ashmead's map of 1833 shows the slow but steady progress that had been made. It marks also the first villa pair, Leny and Rosemont, as already in place and initiating with their suavely elegant Gothic chic, the stately chain of villas that would go up along one side of Clifton Park as the extraordinary length of Vyvyan Terrace took shape between 1832 and 1848 on the other side. Clifton Park was intended as a *rus in urbe* with trees scattered between villas and it remains exactly that.

The contrast between the terraces by Foster, a Barbon of the architectural world, and the villas of Dyer is almost painful. Each Foster terrace unit plods solidly along, separated from its neighbour by a plain Doric pilaster or, in Clifton Vale where the houses have to drop down very steeply, by two pilasters used as steps. This is the old classical reserve which he inherited via his father from the Patys and it is saved from tedium only by the excellence of the ironwork with its essentially superficial Greek trim. There was to be nothing else as sober in fashionable parts of the city.

Where Foster grudged an invention, Dyer was unstinting with his detail and innovation. The typical Dyer villa is not a mere entrance facade to impress a visitor but a three-dimensional structure to be walked around and appreciated from all sides. In revolt against the predictability of the classical roofline, Dyer indulged (and indulgence was the essence of his style) in aediculae: strange little pedimented blocks, often four to a parapet, and in massive panels incised with the Greek key pattern. Tripartite windows thrust out into bold rectangular bays, sometimes two storeys high, were another innovation that was to be copied eagerly. There are free-standing Tower of the Winds, Ionic and Corinthian orders, but the controlling regulators to the facades remain Dyer's favourite duo of flat Doric pilasters. That again became a standard Clifton feature, even the Fosters picked it up.

Edgecumbe with its angular loggia and Kingston prowing its corner site with a tight two-storey bow were not easy models to follow but the middle pair: Widcombe and Bedford, took Clifton's fancy.[2] Clarence Villas (numbers 1 and 2) on Clifton Park is a near replica though with conservative modifications to the windows which suggest that Dyer may not himself have been the architect. This was built in 1836. Next door stands the Aldbourne Villa pair, a more radical adaptation of the Dyer prototype but still visibly indebted to it.[3] The first occupant of the left-hand villa was James Gibbs senior, a brass founder and oil of vitriol manufacturer. He moved in during 1846 and by that date architects were becoming more cavalier in their treatment of the cornice, but the discipline of the dual pilasters still holds firm. As late as the 1860s, the pair on Whiteladies Road next to Victoria Methodist Chapel is still a recognisable version of the Dyer original with the addition of Underwood-style round bay windows.

Vyvyan Terrace, though early, presented fewer models to copy. A terrace is a serious undertaking, often a quick road to bankruptcy, and Vyvyan's awesome length, 57 bays in all, will have served more often as a model to avoid than one to copy. Richard Shackleton Pope, the very name is more appropriate to a consortium than to an ordinary mortal, must have taken to heart the lines from Robert Browning's *Andrea del Sarto*:

> Ah, but a man's reach should exceed his grasp,
> Or what's a heaven for?

But no amount of strong mouldings carved between the first and second floor windows can give a satisfying unity to a structure that could easily have been divided up into five separate terraces.

Pope and Dyer worked in a rewardingly balanced opposition over these Clifton years. Pope was always eager to penetrate a space with deep recessions. The Royal Colonnade, Dorset and Alva Villas, Apsley Terrace, Vyvyan, Buckingham Place and numbers 1, 3, 5, and 7 Richmond Park Road, mark the progress of his obsession. If Pope had to set a demarcation point between houses he preferred a narrow indentation as on Buckingham Place, the Richmond Park houses and Avonside on The Promenade. Dyer liked to add extra details to the outside of an original box. The different nature of the two men is perfectly illustrated in the two ecclesiastical buildings which they put up within a year or two of each other in Clifton. Dyer's Christ Church takes pure, scholarly details from Salisbury Cathedral and puts them together in a classic whole: mainstream, correct and Anglican as a reedy choirboy's treble.[4] Pope's Buckingham Chapel for the Baptists is in every sense nonconformist, though symmetrical. It stands like a demonstration of religious rage, with a loud cry in every jagged pinnacle.

Not that Pope was incapable of tender episodes. The first sector of Vyvyan to be built (14-17) seems to have been his favourite. Buckingham Place, built in 1844, is almost identical except for the ground floor windows. One episode of tenancy connected with number 17 Vyvyan serves as a warning to the pitfalls attendant upon dating these buildings. Although it was begun, as its final name suggests, in 1832, the year when Sir Richard Vyvyan triumphed corruptly at the hustings, the terrace was for many years referred to as a set of numbers in Clifton Park. In 1836, when the house had already been empty for four years though probably not fitted up, a Miss Cormack took number 17. She set up a Ladies Boarding School there in the terrace and lived alone with her girls for eight years in the midst of a building site. Only in 1844 was she joined by Mrs. Hassard at number 16 and an attorney, Mr. Baker, at 15. It is probably a coincidence but single women and widows were often the first to move into new buildings in Clifton, a pointer perhaps to women's financial status. A Miss Glegg was first into Lansdown Place in 1844 and Miss Lyon into Clarence Villas in 1836.

As the inner spaces of Clifton began to fill up the prime site of them all, The Promenade overlooking the Gorge and Leigh Woods, added grand house to grand house marking more clearly than anywhere else the dangers as well as the rewards of stylistic freedom. Dyer's Camp House as usual, had been the first down that physical and metaphorical slope in 1831, overtly classical and templar though playing fast and loose with columnar intervals. Next came Avonhurst in 1836. This actually mocks a temple portico by pretending to support one on applied round arches that clearly support nothing. The effect is witty and dramatic but the game itself is dangerous. Inevitably Pope got in on this prestigious act. His Avonside (now Taylor Maxwell House) was next in 1839. Ten years before at the side of Smirke's Council House on Corn Street Pope had tried out fluted Doric columns *in antis*. Now he delivered three sets for good measure, put in two of his favourite small pediments to top narrow tower-like wings and covered the highly unconvincing remainder of the elevation with a shuffle of his favourite recessed planes. The Greek clock is beginning to unwind.

Sundon (Promenade House) was occupied in 1841 and, though a house of enormous and deliberate presence, it is stylistically nondescript. Everything, capitals, windows, viewing room is overscaled like a giant toy. It draws the eye out but then offers very little. It is to be earnestly hoped that Dyer, working himself by that time towards an early grave, was not the architect, but its three-dimensional qualities and those vast capitals suggest that he could well have been responsible.

And that, to all intents, is the end. Evor House of 1850 is ashlared but featureless apart from Ionic columns *in antis* where a porch should be. After Evor the rough red rubble of Pennant stone becomes standard and designs are hard to pick out from the confusion of surfaces. The collapse of classicism in Clifton after the mid-fifties is a phenomenon never adequately explained. What exactly did the owners of Pembroke Road, Apsley Road, Beaufort Road and all those other expensive, cheerless suburban ways think they were evoking with their Pennant walls and fussy architraves?

162

Back in the 1830s stylistic chains, though loosening, were still in place and productively stimulating. The hold of classicism was far more apparent where a public building was concerned. Pope's Royal Western Hotel, built 1837–8, was the first of these. Now Brunel House and looking grandiloquent and a little foolish across that dull hollow of car parks behind the new Council House, it was intended to preside with authority over the transmit of passengers from the GWR terminus which was meant to stand where the cars now park. I. K. Brunel is supposed to have worked together with Pope on the design, an unlikely combination, but the four-storey elevation does give the impression that one architect designed the top two storeys while the other, with little reference to his partner, prepared the bottom two. As usual there is the effect of interpenetrating spaces.

It would probably have infuriated him if he had been told but Pope was actually much better at small buildings or small effects on larger structures than at giants like Vyvyan and the Royal Western. His church for the Irvingites of 1839, now St. Mary's on the Quay, works perfectly within the restricting templar discipline with just a hint of movement in the secretive blank walls and blocked windows to the sides and all the attention concentrated upon the Composite capitals where restraint relaxes in deep carving and golden textures of stone.

Dyer's Victoria Rooms are the triumph that he intended and very much needed to set the social machine of Clifton in action. He carved his name and the date 1840 on the portico but maps of 1838 show the Rooms as already complete. The fitting out process was probably lengthy. For anyone with real feeling for the classical orders it is hard to speak moderately about Dyer's great octostyle Corinthian portico. It has the scale that templar fronts need and are rarely given, and it has depth with the detail carved richly and to scale. Viewed from within, the proportions and the high columns seem in strong light almost to swim, and it seems credible that the mystery attributed to their origins in Masonic doctrine might really be true. As usual Dyer gave good measure with four splendid columned facades but three of these are hidden by later houses. Only the octostyle stands free and by its presence pulls the confusion of roads, trees and angled buildings around it into order. Dyer had every right to echo the Emperor Justinian and cry out on the dreary steps of the British Museum: 'Smirke, I have outdone thee'. But of course, being Dyer, he would have been too busy.

It is at this point, rather late in Bristol's development, that Charles Underwood made his mark and immediately revealed his whole nature by his designs for the lodges and the nonconformist chapel in the new Arno's Vale Cemetery. These were built between 1837 and 1840. They were not a propitious introduction for an architect hoping to rebuild his bankrupt fortunes with domestic commissions but they brought out the essential rigidity of the man.

Dyer and Pope both used the classical orders with a spirited impatience. Pope's designs would become, by 1850, vitiated by such attitudes, Dyer's death in 1848 was artistically timely. Underwood was different. He revered the orders and enjoyed their restraint. It can be seen in the grave severity of the stocky Doric porticos to the cemetery lodges. Dyer's octostyle Corinthian raises the spirits; Underwood's Doric tetrastyle sobers them. His integrity was such that when he was required to provide what he would have regarded as a debased design for the West of England Academy in the Queen's Road in 1857, he declined the prestigious commission and let it go to another architect, J. H. Hirst. For that reason the Anglican funeral chapel at Arno's Vale cannot be by Underwood and must be another Dyer masterpiece. Partly ruined by vandals and dark with ivy it is numinous in a Tennysonian way. Its dense cluster of capitals carrying a turret like a Roman mausoleum is a poetic and individual expression of Death, like some fanciful Academy design of the period, improbably realised in stone.

It is easy to do justice to the few public buildings of the period but the real wealth of the time lies in the amazing invention and charm of literally hundreds of villas clustered casually on small estates like Richmond Park and Buckingham Vale. Most of the patrician villas, one stage down from the stately homes strung out along The Promenade, lie between Vyvyan and Worcester Terraces. This was pre-eminently Underwood's domain. In the nick of time he stepped in to stem what had looked like being a Gothic rot spreading from the long-established 1832 Leny pair on the corner with College Road. Leny and its neighbour were designed in bland Regency Gothic with no serious pretensions to mediaeval accuracy. But next door, in 1846, the Scanstone House-Clifton Park Villa pair were put up in a full-blooded Westminster Palace Tudor, symmetrical but alive with mullions, dripstones and chimneys disguised as buttresses. Not to be outdone, the owner of Leny added a sizeable chunk of Raglan Castle to his side elevation.

Charles Underwood quelled all this nonsense in two years. He devised a villa elevation basically symmetrical but with a central, round bow window on two storeys. Being Underwood he strapped his bows down tightly with bands and mouldings, and set a giant order pilaster on each side of it to show that nothing was to be too casual. Finally, with heavy playfulness, he laid paterae at fixed intervals along the cornice. Clifton Park House[5] retains one Underwood elevation intact and though it found no tenant until 1850 it looks, with its rustication, sill-bands and lack of paterae to have been his first effort. The Wolverton-Stoneleigh pair next to the offending Westminster Palace Tudor semi are more relaxed. They also were not occupied until 1850 but these and the two lavish return villas to Worcester Terrace were all in place by 1849, as was the severe box of Dyrham across the road (now the Chamber of Commerce).

Underwood, unlike Dyer, was economical with invention and the two seven-bay return houses are grander versions of Stoneleigh with the extra inducement to buyers of a small first floor balcony on top of a bow. These unusually fine and almost separate returns were intended to lure prospective house owners to buy houses in Worcester Terrace itself, which was also about one third complete in 1849. Terrace houses, provided they could be sold, were the big profit makers as they supported each other structurally and could, with luck, be produced on a kind of conveyor belt.

Unsurprisingly Underwood was out of luck. Four years later no additional work had been done at Worcester. With its implacable array of regimented windows it was a terrace that confronted rather than seduced a buyer. Carved work, apart from mass-produced paterae daisies, was cut to nothing. Before the Art Deco was ever dreamed of Worcester Terrace was its classical apotheosis. Design-wise Underwood was not in tune with his consumers. What Clifton wanted was a terrace like Belgrave of 1851, awash, fore and aft, with ornamental fenestration.

Shadowed by Lansdown Place, another but milder terrace, the villa cluster of Richmond Park Road is casual, imaginative and diverse. Pope appears there at his best, scattering small classical gables on pairs and single houses alike in a preview of the Tudor 1930s, only the black-and-white fake timbering is missing. The two pairs at numbers 1, 3, 5 and 7 are particularly rewarding examples of Pope's attention to detail. He contrived his interpenetration of spaces by a balcony between the wings and supported it on more elaborate versions of the angular columns on those recessed sections of Vyvyan and Worcester. Instead of a lesene he divided each house by a narrow, recessed gully. Then, to prove that he was going determinedly to Victorian seed (the year was 1845), he applied Elizabethan-type diamond decoration right across the elevations by repeating the balcony balustrading under each first floor window. Pope's only constraint was that each house had to cost £500 or more to attract, as it still does, a 'nice' class of person.

The particular charm of the Richmond Park area is its diversity. Fonthill is heavily corniced, numbers 8 and 10 kick over the traces with a guilloche frieze all around their ground floor windows, then make amends by pediments on the first floor. Spring Villa is austere as befitted a house for the minister of the chapel next door. Carlton Terrace was a little earlier, occupied in 1842, cheaper because it was a small terrace, and not by Pope. Its most amazing feature is a wicked neo-Georgian addition of the 1930s. But the real treasure of the neighbourhood is the delicately Soaneian terrace of four houses in Kensington Place. Its ground floor is plain with banded rustication, its attic makes a virtue of alternately blocked windows. All the emphasis lies on the subtle projection and recession of the large tripartite windows on the first floor. This is real architecture achieved without apparent effort.

Looming over all these visual pleasures is Lansdown Place, a thoroughly handsome terrace but a provocative one to the architectural historian as there is no clue to its designer. It was begun in 1842, financed by a Mr. Hemming, and the first tenants were at home in numbers 3–13 in 1845. Apart from a scatter of dual pilasters its elevation plays no tricks and has no idiosyncrasies. The central section and the wings are handsomely advanced and the continuous balcony suggests an architect who had been accustomed to rely on ironwork for relief. Inevitably, Thomas Foster comes to mind, fresh from his heavy labours on The Mall. It was in 1842 that his livelier son John joined the family firm. Also, in its lee on the corner of Richmond Park Road, is a delicate pair of houses (dated 1842) quite unlike anything else in the area, but with bands of anthemion carvings suspiciously like those that the Fosters had applied to the Lower Arcade back in 1824. Spatially, with their curved porches and conservatories on fluted Ionic columns, they are like a throwback to another age, which perhaps clinches a Foster authorship. The right-hand house of the pair, Lansdowne Villa, was first owned by the processor of a patent savoury vinegar, which gives the right social register for the road.

Lansdown Place introduces the curious dead heart of Clifton: Victoria Square; 'dead' in the best sense of the word because it is so quiet, wide enough and leafy enough for its three terraced sides hardly to relate to each other, essentially a pedestrian interlude with a long, diagonal path crossing an area of mature trees. For its spaciousness, Clifton has Mr. Hemming of Lansdown Place to thank. The Merchant Venturers, who owned the land when it was Ferney Close, a cattle pasture, hoped to build either two crescents, one on each side of the already existing diagonal, or a complete new square of four terraces with additional villas at the angles, rather in the way that Albert Villa relates now to the Royal Promenade. Either scheme would have presented the tenants of Lansdown Place with an ugly view of tatty backside buildings. So Mr. Hemming fought, bought or cajoled the Merchants to a standstill.

Finally, despairing of ever seeing a ground rent, the Merchants gave in and on 14 March 1845 told their Superintendent and Receiver for the Clifton estates, Mr. J. Marmont, to mark out the land for the Royal Promenade, thereby leaving Lansdown its open view west-south-west.[6] The Merchants had to subsidise heavily a grumbling and pessimistic contractor, William Bateman Reed, to build the Promenade and bring them eventually, when the last house was sold in August 1853 for around £1,500, a ground rent overall of £200. Because any 19th century building in Bristol of unknown authorship is usually attributed to the Fosters, not only the Royal Promenade but the utterly dissimilar south-west side, a riotous Rundbogen exotic in plummy red stone, have been attributed to the dynamic young John Foster.[7]

There is no mention of the Fosters in the Merchants' Hall Books covering this period and the Hall's careful documentation makes it clear that J. Marmont, who had prepared the earlier crescents and squares, also designed the Royal Promenade. An elaborate drawing signed by Marmont shows a mews that he was proposing to build in exactly the same thunder-cloud, heavy round-arched style as the Promenade itself.[8] With its busy architraves, a nodding cornice to rival the Palazzo Farnese and an attic storey more like a suspended Romanesque cloister, the Royal Promenade was the Italophile's answer to Underwood's fierce minimalism on Worcester Terrace. The south-west side, begun in 1855, was to the signed designs, beautifully drawn and coloured in the Merchants' archives, of John Yalland, builder and contractor of Holton Street, St. Paul's.

Clearly it is unwise to attempt to pigeonhole all the architectural riches of this area under a mere four architects when fourteen of them are listed in the directories of 1840. Buckingham Vale is another small estate of enchantingly diverse, rendered and coloured villa pairs and small terraces after the Cheltenham manner, all built in the mid-1840s. Its flagship is the superbly confident range of Buckingham Villas in Oakfield Road, four pairs decisively outlined by tremendous panelled pilasters, some of whose capitals owe their floral abundance to Dyer's example. One puzzling feature of this eminently inhabitable little estate is the number of bay wreaths that have been carved on its houses. These were usually Pope's private signature on his designs, as on Vyvyan Terrace. The houses began to be occupied in 1849 and in 1850 who should appear resident at number 4 Buckingham Vale but Richard Shackleton Pope himself. It is likely that he and the builders had come to some arrangement of design services in exchange for a price cut. The most celebrated villas are the pair ingeniously contrived within an Ionic temple at the head of Buckingham Vale, which should now be seen as one of Pope's least characteristic designs. The whole group with its complex interrelation of various but wholly harmonious parts exemplifies the partnership between an architect and unsung speculative builders.[9]

There are a number of terraces, not all of them late, in the area where Clifton verges into Cotham along the Whiteladies Road. Vittoria Terrace was begun in 1828 and still survives, mercifully half-hidden by shops as it has a good claim to the title of 'the most graceless classical terrace in Britain'. In complete contrast, just behind it a terrace of four, Melrose Cottages, stands like a simple but satisfying theorem of parts on Cotham village street. With a delicate sub-Soaneian propriety, its broad and narrow single bays are set between stone pilasters, while the entrance bays are more deeply recessed and emphasised at the roofline by miniature arcades. It was an early design, 1843, by George Gay who was still building inventively classical pairs in this area well into the 1860s.

The vintage year for the completion of terraces around Whiteladies Road was 1849. Burlington Buildings, Melrose Terrace, Aberdeen Terrace, South Parade, Leicester Place and Westbourne Place all began to come into occupation then as Clifton's vacant spaces filled and there was a movement towards the line of aristocratic and upper-middle-class villas along the Whiteladies Road itself.[10] Burlington Buildings and South Parade have a massive deliberation and a lack of ornament quite alien to Clifton of the last two decades. Easily the most distinguished terrace is Aberdeen, also the most odd. Its pediment is boldly framed but deliberately blunted to give it three sides instead of the usual two, and its conventional balustrading is varied by panels carved with Union Jacks! The firm double projection of the central feature, the rusticated ground floor with arched windows and the first floor of tripartite windows balconied with slim spears of ironwork gives a terrace of single-bay houses all the consequence of one with much larger units.

Even out here Richard Pope was active. His Brighton Park, or numbers 30–40 Whiteladies Road, was an experiment on the Prince's Buildings theme of semi-detached pairs claiming both individuality and unity in a terrace form. For Pope it had the advantage of allowing him to set a gable or pediment (the correct term is arguable) over each house. But what he designed at this time for Leicester Place on

167

the St. Paul's Road was rather less happy, even a little disturbing, as it underlines the moral that even the best intentioned of libertarian indulgences end in a state indistinguishable from decadence.

At Leicester Place the classical free-form that produced such rich diversity in Clifton, has become mere scrabbling about for ways to attract attention. The windows lurch uneasily from side to side as they climb the facades; the frieze is a pleasant doodle on the lines of that ominous Elizabethan balustrade on Pope's two 1845 pairs in Richmond Park Road; the pilaster strips miss their apparent aim at the doors and end in a loose flap of carving.[11] The whole terrace provokes the uneasy speculation that if this was the price of aesthetic freedom then there must have been potent arguments in favour of chains. The architect of Vyvyan Terrace was also responsible in later life for many of the solemn, styleless houses that line Pembroke Road.

Terraces were, by their nature, a quest for a cheaper line of building. Standards of villa design in this eastern fringe tended to hold up longer. There are two astonishingly fine George Gay return elevations, one at the top of Cotham Hill and another at the corner of Cotham Brow with Cotham Grove. Both employ the full range of those devices that Charles Dyer introduced in 1832 with Tower of the Winds capitals, dual pilasters and semicircular porches, but add to these great screens of ironwork of an almost New Orleans lavishness and some of Underwood's light semicircular bows.

Finally, at the foot of Cotham Brow, where Arley Hill turns off, there is perched a great, gaunt wreck of a double villa by William Armstrong that sums up all the experimental daring of Bristol classicism in these, its last but greatest days, and all the city's subsequent indifference to what was achieved. The heads of the Ionic capitals on its porch have been shattered. One truly giant pilaster on its side wall has fallen away leaving the spreading acanthus leaves of its capital suspended over peeling plaster. There still remains enough from the wreathed acroteria of its parapets down through the wide symmetries of the windows in their arched recession to assert a weary dignity far above its actual status.

That was the real merit of this last episode in Bristol's hitherto cautious progression through classicism. For just these few decades a conservative city took risks and a conscious, dangerous delight, not only in proportion but in overt display. What is left still provokes and visually enriches those who live in its houses and those who pass them in their ordinary journeys. What began so faint and muted down in Queen Square ended up here on the hills in a whole blast of trumpets.

CHAPTER SEVEN – NOTES

1 Quoted in Latimer, *Nineteenth Century*, p.167.
2 Kingston's bow may, however, have inspired Charles Underwood's similar bow windows on Clifton Park House, Stoneleigh and the Worcester Terrace return houses.
3 This pair is sometimes confusingly labelled simply Rosemont which is an error as the real Rosemont is one of the Gothic pair with Leny and was first occupied in 1841 by the Rev. Edward Young.
4 The tower and spire, though later, are plausibly claimed to be to Dyer's original design.
5 Not, it should be noted, Clifton Park Villa. Clifton Park House stands opposite Leny-Rosemont on the corner of College Road. Clifton Park Villa is wildly Gothic.
6 Merchant Venturers' Hall Book 20, p.106.
7 Jenner, p.260 and p.261 respectively.
8 This drawing is dated 14 April 1849 and comes from the firm, Marmont and Lloyd Architects, which had been set up in 15 Corn Street in 1847.
9 A similar Cheltonian group of rendered and stone houses grew up in the 1840s behind Harley Terrace.
10 A fine pair with all the hallmarks of Underwood's style, Cradley House and Tanworth House, survive at the corner with St. Paul's Road.
11 At Codrington Place, however, built in 1852, two years later, the newly formed partnership of Pope, Bindon and Clark proved that it still had tremendous inventive resources when the money was right and the scale modest.

169

Edgcumbe and Thornton, by Dyer (1832). Almost every device of later Clifton classicism features on this expensive pair.

Widcombe, 1832. This particular arrangement of aediculae and twin pilasters would be much copied.

First occupied in 1846, this villa pair on Clifton Park plays a cheerful mannerist game with features borrowed from Widcombe.

Dyer's judgement, essential classicism and eclectic range is most perfectly expressed in Gothic Christ Church, begun 1841.

The demure delicacy of Buckingham Place (1844) and the symmetrical religious rage of the Chapel, designed in 1842, exemplify Pope's fatal ability.

Vyvyan Terrace by Pope of 1832-47. The three houses on the right were built first with all Pope's delight in interpenetrated spaces.

Avonhurst on The Promenade (1836). Italianate in its wings, Grecian in its central bays and witty in its fake round arches.

Avonside, 1839. With Pope's favourite gabled pediments, columns *in antis*, wreaths and recessed planes, Victorianism is imminent but not arrived.

Designed by Charles Dyer in 1832, completed in 1840, the Conservative (later Victoria) Rooms were the social and aesthetic cathedral of classical Clifton.

Dyer's Anglican funeral chapel at Arno's Vale, like something raised in the late Empire out on the Appian Way.

This villa pair (1846) in Palace of Westminster Tudor, almost cracked the classical mould of Clifton Park.

A return of 1849 to Worcester Terrace with Charles Underwood's grudging concessions to ornament.

With minimal ornament and negligible charm, an ageing Grecian like Underwood provoked the reaction of Victorian eclecticism – Worcester Terrace, building in 1849.

The subtle complexity of this pair in Richmond Park Road (1846) catches Pope poised between classicism and a seductive Jacobethan.

Kensington Place, 1846 – a terrace that represents best the freedom and the restraint of the Clifton renaissance.

With Lansdown Place of 1842–5, Thomas Foster and Son cautiously updated the image of a conservative firm.

Designed by Marmont, built by Bateman Reed, the Royal Promenade, begun 1845, introduced a heavy, alien exoticism to Clifton.

An idyll of speculative builders' classicism in Buckingham Vale, 1847–9, designed with some help from Pope.

Clifton classicism scaled down to the village street without loss of form: Melrose Cottages, Cotham Hill of 1843 by George Gay. Aberdeen Terrace of 1849 marks a return of confidence with bold projections, acanthus capitals and single-bay houses grandly scaled.

185

A heritage neglected – William Armstrong's house on Cotham Brow; the superb
detail is repeated and still intact on the other side.

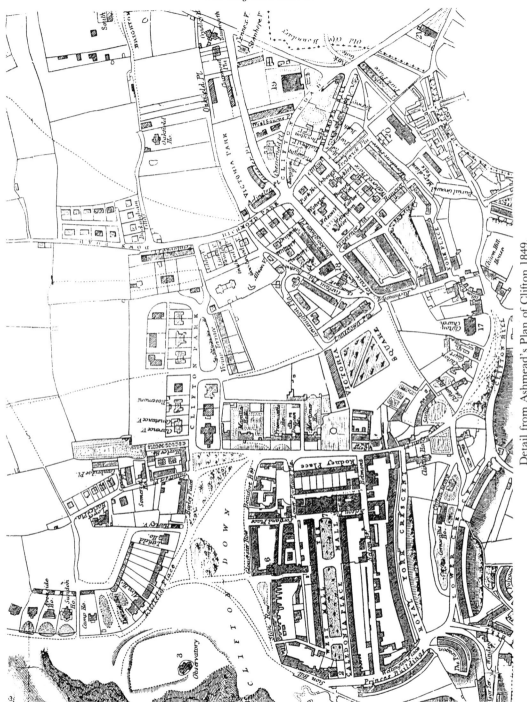

Detail from Ashmead's Plan of Clifton 1849.

Glossary

ACANTHUS: A fleshy leaved plant conventionalized in the decoration of classical capitals.

ANTAE: Flat PILASTERS at either end of a row of columns.

ANTHEMION: Ornament in Greek architecture resembling honeysuckle often incorporated with ACANTHUS.

ARTISAN MANNERISM: A non-courtly style of architecture of the seventeenth century in which elements of Elizabethan, Jacobean, Mannerist and Classical styles are used indiscriminately.

ARTS AND CRAFTS: Movement in the late nineteenth century inspired by the teaching of William Morris and Ruskin, to revive handicrafts and improve standards of design.

ASHLAR: Masonry walling made of large smooth even blocks.

ASTYLAR: Term describing a facade without PILASTERS or columns.

BAROQUE: Movement of the seventeenth and early eighteenth centuries. Architecture characterised by exuberant decoration and massing and complex composition.

BAY: Compartment or section in a building marked on the outside by windows, inside by columns.

CARYATID: Sculptured female figure used in Greek architecture instead of a column to support an ENTABLATURE, loosely, columns and pilasters, carved wholly or partly in human form.

CORINTHIAN: See ORDERS.

CORNICE: Projecting horizontal section at top of ENTABLATURE, also any projecting ornamental moulding crowning an external facade or internally at junction of wall and ceiling.

COVE: Large concave moulding especially that produced by the arched junction of wall and ceiling.

CUPOLA: A small dome on a circular or polygonal base crowning a roof or turret, frequently used to light a staircase.

DADO: Usually the finishing of the lower part of an interior wall from floor to waist height, often decorated with a frieze or similar device.

DENTIL: A small square block used in series in IONIC, CORINTHIAN, and more rarely, DORIC cornices.

DORIC: See ORDERS.

ELEVATION: The external faces of a building; also used to mean a drawing made in projection on a vertical plane to show any one face of a building.

ENTABLATURE: Upper part of an ORDER consisting of ARCHITRAVE, FRIEZE and CORNICE.

FOLLY: A deliberately functionless building or ruined structure, popular in the eighteenth century to add an element of the picturesque to the landscape.

GIBBS SURROUND: The surround of a doorway or window made up of alternately large and small blocks of stone, named after the architect James Gibbs.

GOTHICK: Eighteenth century use of Gothic forms to create a Romantic mood in a building without recourse to Gothic precepts of design.

GOTHIC REVIVAL: Movement to revive the Gothic style belonging chiefly to the eighteenth and nineteenth centuries. Distinguished from Gothick by a more correct archaeological use of motifs.

GROTTO: Man made and highly stylized cave, popular in the eighteenth century as a feature in the gardens of country houses.

IN ANTIS: See PORTICO.

ITALIANATE: Nineteenth century revivalist style of architecture evoking Renaissance Italy.

KEYSTONE: The central stone of an arch or rib vault.

LOGGIA: A Gallery open on one or more sides, sometimes pillared; it may also be a separate structure, usually in a garden.

NEO-CLASSICAL: A term describing the architecture of a movement which began in the 1750s as a return to the principles of Greek or Roman Art and Architecture.

OGEE ARCH: A pointed arch made up of two curves, each of which is made up of a convex and concave part.

ORDERS: In classical architecture a system of architectural design comprising a column with base, shaft, and capital supporting an entablature. The whole ornamented according to five ordained styles: DORIC, TUSCAN, IONIC, CORINTHIAN or COMPOSITE. GIANT ORDER – an order where the columns rise from the ground through two or more storeys.

PALLADIAN: In English architecture, the classical style of the Italian architect Andrea Palladio, introduced by Inigo Jones in the early seventeenth century, and later made popular by Lord Burlington

and his followers.

PATERA: A circular ornament sunk into a wall, decorated with stylized foliage or petals.

PEDIMENT: Originally a low pitched triangular GABLE over a PORTICO used in classical architecture and frequently used later to decorate doorways and windows. BROKEN PEDIMENT – one in which the apex of the triangle is removed, leaving a roughly arc-like shape though other shapes are possible. SEGMENTAL PEDIMENT – one made of an arc of a circle, almost always used over doors or windows.

PIANO NOBILE: An Italian renaissance term, signifying the principal floor of a house containing the reception rooms, the whole raised on a basement storey.

PILASTER: A flat column set against the surface of a building, built into it and projecting not more than one third of its surface breadth.

PORTICO: A roofed structure supported by columns, attached to a building normally as an entrance feature. PORTICO IN ANTIS – One in which the columns are in a plane with the walls of the building i.e. the PORTICO does not project beyond the building. A HEXASTYLE portico is one with six columns. A TETRASTYLE portico is one with four columns.

QUATREFOIL: A four-lobed ornament used mainly in Gothic architecture, as a surface decoration, also found in window tracery.

QUOINS: Dressed stones at the corner of a building, sometimes imitated by groups of brick in wholly brick buildings.

REGENCY: The style of architecture prevalent under George IV as King

1820-1830 or as Prince Regent 1811-1820, epitomised by the works of John Nash.

ROCOCO: A very ornate, light, mid-eighteenth century style of art and architecture, following the more weighty BAROQUE. In England it was mainly confined to interior design, plasterwork and furniture, while a PALLADIAN style was almost exclusively used for the exterior of major buildings.

RUSTICATION: The use of massive elements of masonry mainly in the basement storey of a building, to give an impression of strength. Originally the blocks were rough hewn; in later styles the surface would be smooth with artifically large courses cut between the blocks.

VERMICULATED RUSTICATION: the surface of the rusticated blocks is heavily channelled with curved, irregular grooves, giving an impression of the surface being riddled with worms.

STRING COURSE: A projecting course of stone or brick running horizontally across a building.

VENETIAN WINDOW: A classical window made up of three parts, the central part wider and taller than the other two and arched. Also used for doorways.

VITRUVIAN SCROLL: A repeated classical motif made up of features reminiscent of waves terminated by scrolls.

VOLUTE: A spiral scroll used in the IONIC capital. Also used as a linking motif in classical architecture.

Select Bibliography

Barker, Kathleen, *The Theatre Royal Bristol 1766–1966* (1974).

Barrett, William, *The History and Antiquities of the City of Bristol*, 1798: facsimile reprint (Gloucester, 1982).

Brewer, James Norris, *Delineations of Gloucestershire* (1825–7).

The Bristol Memorialist (Bristol, 1823).

Busby, Charles, *A Series of Designs for Villas and Country Houses* (1808).

Charlton, J. & Milton, D.M. *Redland 791–1800* (Bristol, 1951).

Colvin, Howard Montague, *A Biographical Dictionary of British Architects 1600–1840* (1978).

Crook, Joe Mordaunt, *The Greek Revival: Neo-Classical Attitudes in British Architecture 1760–1870* (1972).

Cruickshank, Dan & Burton, Neil, *Life in the Georgian City* (1990).

Dening, C. F. W. *The Eighteenth-Century Architecture of Bristol* (Bristol, 1923).

Ellis, M. H. *Francis Greenway: His Life and Times* (Sydney, 1949).

Gibbs, James, *A Book of Architecture Containing Designs of Buildings and Ornaments* (1728).

Gill, Jennifer, *The Bristol Scene: Views of Bristol by Bristol Artists from the Collection of the Art Gallery* (Bristol, 1973).

Girouard, Mark, *Life in the English Country House* (1978).

Girouard, Mark, *The English Town* (1990).

Halfpenny, William, *The Art of Sound Building* (1725).

Halfpenny, William, *Perspective Made Easy* (1731).

Halfpenny, William, *Andrea Palladio's First Book of Architecture* (1751).

Halfpenny, William & Halfpenny, John, *Chinese and Gothic Architecture Properly Ornamented* (1752).

Halfpenny, William, *The Modern Builder's Assistant* (1757).

Harris, Eileen, *British Architectural Writers 1556–1785* (Cambridge, 1990).

Harris, John, *The Palladians* (1981).

Hayward, Helena, *Thomas Johnson and English Rococo* (1964).

Hussey, Christopher, *English Country Houses: Early Georgian 1715–1760* (1955).

Ison, Walter, *The Georgian Buildings of Bristol*, 2nd. revised edition (Bath, 1978).

Jenner, Michael, Gomme, Andor, & Little, Bryan, *Bristol: an architectural history* (1979).

Johnson, Thomas, *One Hundred and Fifty New Designs* (1758).

Jones, Barbara, *Follies and Grottoes*, 2nd revised edition (1974).

Jones, Rev. Emlyn, *Our Parish of Mangotsfield* (reprinted edition, Bath, 1979).

Ladd, Frederick J. *Architects at Corsham Court* (Bradford-on-Avon, 1978).

Latimer, John, *Annals of Bristol: Volume 2, Eighteenth Century* (Bristol, 1970).

Latimer, John, *Annals of Bristol in the Nineteenth Century* (Bristol, 1887).

Malcolm, James P. *First Impressions or Sketches from Art and Nature Animate & Inanimate* (1807).

Mathews, W. *New History, Survey and Description of the City and Suburbs of Bristol and Guide to the Hotwells and Clifton* (Bristol, 1793).

McGrath, Patrick, *The Merchant Venturers of Bristol* (1975).

Mellor, Penelope, *A Kingsdown Community* (Bristol, 1985).

191

Mellor, Penelope, *A Kingsdown Collection* (Bristol, 1987).

Mowl, Tim & Earnshaw, Brian, *John Wood: Architect of Obsession* (Bath, 1988).

Mowl, Tim, *Bristol: Last Age of the Merchant Princes* (Bath, 1991).

Pevsner, Nikolaus, *The Buildings of England: North Somerset and Bristol* (1958).

Powell, A.G. *Bristol Commercial Rooms 1811–1951* (Bristol, 1951).

Rococo: Art and Design in Hogarth's England, Victorian & Albert Museum Exhibition Catalogue (1984).

Skelton, Joseph, *Engravings of the Antiquities of Bristol* (Bristol, 1831).

Southern, Richard, *The Georgian Playhouse* (1948).

Stembridge, P. K. *Goldney a House and a Family* (Bristol, 1969).

Stoddard, Sheena, *Mr Braikenridge's Brislington* (Bristol, 1981).

Summerson, John, *Architecture in Britain 1530–1830* revised edition, (1983).

Summerson, John, *Georgian London*, 2nd edition (1962).

Tilling, A. E. *Guide to Arno's Castle*, no date.

Verey, David, *The Buildings of England: Gloucestershire I The Cotswolds* (1970).

Horace Walpole's Correspondence, edited by W. S. Lewis (Oxford, 1973).

Ware, Isaac, *A Complete Body of Architecture* (1756).

Wood, John, *An Essay towards a Description of Bath*, 1742; revised edition of 1765 (reprinted, Bath, 1969).

Index of Architects, Craftsmen and Builders

Index of Buildings